Celeste Ball May

**Sounds of the Prairie**

Celeste Ball May

**Sounds of the Prairie**

ISBN/EAN: 9783744677592

Printed in Europe, USA, Canada, Australia, Japan

Cover: Foto ©Thomas Meinert / pixelio.de

More available books at **www.hansebooks.com**

# SOUNDS OF THE PRAIRIE

BY

## CELESTE MAY

———

TOPEKA KANSAS

GEO. W. CRANE & CO. PRINTERS AND BINDERS

1886

# DEDICATION.

## I.

Accept, dear parents, in token of my love,
This little book of poems—fancies trove
    From out my leisure hours.
And if your approbation they secure,
'Twill all my trepidation reassure,
    And strew my path with flowers.


Through love of thee, 'twas first I tried to write,
Hoping I might some pleasing lines indite,
    As proof of my deep love.
And, if I can your hearts and ears delight,
I shall be always glad I tried to write,
    Expressing filial love.


Begun, it seemed the outlet long desired,
To vent the deepest thoughts my soul acquired,
    And longed to give expression;
Impressions that were near akin to pain,
Till they were made to live in words again—
    Words' true and highest mission.

Each separate life its own experience lives,
Yet all have much in common — and it gives,
     Pleasure to relate it.
The poet should his own life understand,
And every phase of life in the broad land,
     And truly should depict it.


II.

In the quiet and seclusion of my country home,
Many pleasant fancies of the past and future
    come —
     A past-time most unique:
And if I can awaken, in one sad heart, the thrill
Of pleasures long forgotten — then I shall fulfill
     The mission that I seek:


Or reproduce to memory the trials bravely stood,
Inducing faith in the prophecy, that "All things
    good
     Come to those who wait"—
Then I shall be happy, and very well repaid
For these simple rhymes, and the effort I have
    made
     To enter Fancy's gate.


In "Sounds of the Prairie," it is my aspiration,
As one who witnessed it, to give an adumbra-
    tion
     Of the pioneer's privation.

In others I have sought to faithfully portray
Lessons learned around us in things of every day—
      Of every caste and station.


On the stormy sea of letters, I launch my little
    boat,
Wondering if it will sink, or sail, or float,
      When loosened from its moorings.
Like a bird, I send this fledgling forth from the
    nest,
Longing, yet dreading, to send it on its quest
      With untried wings.


Yet of one thing I feel very confident—
You, who always were so lenient
      With my childish faults and failures,
Will surely judge as kindly now, of these,
My very first attempt my friends to please,
      In soft and rythmic measures.

# SOUNDS OF THE PRAIRIE.

Muse of all the Gifts and Graces!
  Though the fields around us wither,
There are ampler realms and spaces,
Where no foot has left its traces:
  Let us turn and wander thither!
               *—Longfellow.*

## THE PIONEER.

"MARY," said John Calhoun, on one bright summer morn,
As he was starting to plow his rented field of
  corn,
"If you are willing, we will westward go this
  fall,
Where the proceeds of my hard labor we shall
  reap all.
And we can make us a home, while the children
  are yet small,
Which will always do us honor—one which we
  all,
While they are still about us, will greatly enjoy;
And it will our youthful time and energies employ.
It is very hard to get a start back here, you
  know,
Where on another's land we must always reap
  and sow."

And Mary, with a sinking and throbbing at her
    heart,
For the old associations from which she'd have
    to part,
Gave quick assent; for she was always ready
To sacrifice herself, and unselfishly to study
For the good of others; though much more she
    would renounce,
Than e'er her husband dreamed; for much more
    a woman counts
The love of home and friends than does the
    manly heart,
Which, ever here and yonder, contentedly, can
    dart;
Nor is so closely bound by early ties and pleas-
    ure,
But thinks the great round world but suited to
    his measure.


And so, while he industriously his crops at-
    tended,
She busily sewed, devised, repaired and neatly
    mended
Their clothes and household goods; and made
    all preparation,
To be in readiness for the long privation
She knew they must endure, in changing their
    location.
The odds and ends of work were brought unto
    completion; .

The last quilt quilted, and woven the new rag
    carpet gay —
Work of the thrifty housewife's hands for many
    a day.
For though to far-off western prairies they were
    going,
She thought, 'mong needful things, some beauty
    of bestowing.


At last the day set for their departure was at
    hand;
Ready the great, stout team and the covered
    wagon stand,
Equipped for the long journey; and the hour of
    parting
From father, mother, sister, brother and friends,
    starting
Away from so much they had loved and prized
    before —
'Twas as if on all their former lives they'd shut
    the door —
Beginning life in a new country, with new
    friends;
Where success on their own pluck and energy
    depends:
So the first real grief she'd ever known was thus
    entailed,
But love for those who nearest were at last pre-
    vailed.

2

Within their roomy wagon, they had stowed
    away
The things they most would need for many a
    long day;
For little time or means to purchase them again
They'd have, when far out on their homestead
    claim; and then
It would seem more like home to have the self-
    same things,
For fond association to all our home things
    clings.
Tied on top the feed box, was a coop of Ply-
    mouth Rock fowls;
The house dog, too, is with them, and at ap-
    proach of intrusion growls.
And slowly led along, as if she were loth to go,
Tied to the wagon, the favorite cow, soft-eyed
    and slow.

For weeks, slowly but steadily westward they
    kept their way;
Camping at night, weary, but feeling that every
    day
Brought them nearer to their longed-for destina-
    tion.
For the children, the travel and camp fires were
    pleasant recreation;
And all enjoyed the victuals cooked on the glow-
    ing coals
Of a fire that's nearly burned—built in little
    scraped-out holes

In the ground. The fragrant, steaming coffee,
and the bowls
Of delicious bread and milk, refreshed their
weary souls;
And just as sweet their sleep, in the wagon or on
the ground,
As ever it was in their beds at home — and just
as sound.

Beyond the marts of men, wilder grew the scene
And fewer the habitations; many miles would
intervene
Between the towns. And on every side, like a
smooth-waved sea,
A beautiful view, lay the clean-grassed, undulat-
ing, western prairie.
A little further on, and they began the pleasant
task
Of choosing a location — one as fine as they
could ask,
They were not long in finding; and at once they
set to work
To build a house upon it, for hard work they
would not shirk.
And first, the breaking plow was called in requi-
sition,
Turning the sod in a square, about the chosen
position.

Not long were John's strong arms in laying up
the sod

In four straight walls; while Mary and the chil-
    dren stood
Approvingly—giving the assistance that they
    could.
And then, for covering it, he sought the scanty
    wood,
Found a tree well suited to his purpose, quickly
Felled, loaded, and hauled home; where he most
    deftly
Constructed from its branches a great beam and
    rafters;
These he thatched with willows, and covered
    with sod.   After
Some delay and much hard work, he procured
A shelter that seemed a home, after all they had
    endured,
In living in their wagon, or under the broad,
    blue sky.
For windows and doors they must wait, for there
    was no place nigh
Where they could be procured, till a well was
    dug and walled,
And then he'd drive a distance back which
    would have appalled
A man less resolute, and buy the windows and
    doors,
The supplies for the winter, and lumber for the
    floors.
Hard he worked, and steady, but late it was in
    the fall,
Before he found time to plaster the black, un-
    gainly wall;

Then laid was the bright rag carpet, and hung
    the curtains white;
The snowy bed in one corner—in the other the
    stove so bright.

A few bright prints they had brought, hung on
    the whitewashed wall;
And white muslin for the ceiling hung high
    above it all.
With real appreciation, and satisfaction keen,
They viewed the work of their hands—proud as
    any king or queen;
For, though without 'twas homely, it was all
    their own;
Within, in thrifty tidiness, its home-like comfort
    shone.
And here, reluctantly, we'll leave them—feeling
    sure
Such enterprise as they possess will still endure
The hardships incident to life on the frontier.
Prosperity, and health, and wealth, we wish
    them, here.

## THE PRAIRIE FIRE.

### IN THE FALL OF 1878.

AFTER dinner, one October day,
A merry group sat chatting,
In a large stone house by the creek;
Each one telling, in his way,
Of where he had been living,
And the home he had come to seek,
On this wide and beautiful prairie.


One had taken this claim, another that;
Each dwelling on the merits of his piece,
And his good fortune in securing it:
And thus, in pleasant converse, long they sat—
The several families who had procured a lease
Of this, the only house for miles about it,
Until afforded time to build their homes—


Nor dreamed of fast-approaching ill.
At length—"'Tis Indian summer," one re-
    marked,
"And we must to work, this autumn weather,
Or our fond hopes we'll not fulfill,
In this enterprise in which we are embarked:"
And so their group was broken up.  Thither,
Each one started to his work.

Said another, on reaching the out-door air,
"'Tis the smokiest Indian summer, I declare,
I ever saw — must be where they're manufac-
tured."
And another—"'Tis the smoke from a prairie
fire!
And we must fight with zeal and ire!
But be assured,
The women and children are safe, right here;
So let them stay and have no fear,
For all around the house 'tis clear
Of grass, and has only the clippings from
stone."

Away they went, on horses fleet,
With buckets, and sacks, and all things meet,
Hoping to make the fight complete,
And save the winter's grazing.
The women, with white and ashen face,
Brought the carriages and cattle to the place
About the house, for safety.
But prairie life in this new phase,
Was not one designed to raise
Their high opinion of it.

An Indian scare they had just passed through;
Expecting, hourly, nobody knew
How many, or when
Some of the bloodthirsty clan
Would their scalps appraise
And their dwellings raze—

But rumor ran,
That there were thousands — and the van
Was close at hand.


Many for safety sought the nearest fort;
Others, together, sought support
In numbers.
They of whom we write declared they'd stand
On their own land,
And try to save
The few possessions that they have,
And just as they thought the fiends all passed,
And began to breathe free again, at last,
Some of the stragglers of the band,
With savage heart and cruel hand —
Mad at the soldiers — lit the brand
Which desolated so much land.


Dark and darker grew the sky!
The roar and crackle soon were nigh,
The flames and smoke ascending high,
In spite of all their efforts.
Two great burning lines of flame —
One on either side the creek —
Swiftly, madly, onward came,
As if all things it would seek;
Crackling, roaring, wildly rushing
Over tree and shrub, devouring
Every obstacle in its way —
Nothing could its fury stay.

While, far back
In its blackened track,
Smouldered the back-fires sullenly.
And here and there
The lurid glare
Showed some new place, or pasture fair,
A victim to its ravages.

Fearful it was, and grand!
In awe the women stand,
Watching the burning land,
From their safe shelter;
And yet in deep suspense
For those, who, in defense,
Had gone to fight it.

Exhausted, breathless, cinder-blackened,
Seeing their efforts vain,
The men now slackened
Their arduous fight;
And the fire, in its resistless reign,
Swept on, with ruin in its train —
Terrific in its might.
Sometimes, the side-fires they had held at bay,
Thinking its dreaded havoc thus to stay,
Only to retreat at last and give full sway;
For fire, on such a windy day,
Is an enemy with vantage.

Next day, for miles and miles around,
Naught but the bare and blackened ground
Could anywhere be seen.

All the broad acres of nutritious grass,
With which the winter they had hoped to pass
Without much need of feed,
Were swept away by its greed.
And glad were they when the snow, so white,
Hid the blackened prairie away from sight.

## THE SNOW.

At first it tossed wildly about in the air,
Uncertain if it were to lodge here, or there,
Angrily beating like beast in its lair—
Penetrating everywhere;
Blinding and driving all in its way,
That fiercely cold, bleak winter's day;
And man or beast that chanced to roam
Far from shelter or from home,
Losing his way, was afterward found,
Frozen and dead, in a snowy mound.

After its first mad fury was spent,
Settling in quiet and content,
It made the earth, so black and bare,
A picture of beauty and pureness fair,
Glistening in the moonlight like jewels rare.
And many weeks, in its mantle of snow,
The earth lay enwrapped, as if to show
A pity for its bareness.

All there seemed in existence was a sea of
    snow;
The sky overhead, and naught below
But the pure, and cold, and crystalled snow.
And like a lone ship in the midst of the sea,
The little stone house, so dear to me —
The blue smoke curling upward from its chim-
    ney,
Looked our homestead on the smooth, white
    prairie.


Beautiful thought it was, and grand.
Great inconvenience, on every hand,
Was endured by the hardy pioneer;
Almost unable was he to steer
The ship of home through safely, here,
Away from roads and all supplies,
Under the cold and wintry skies.


Indeed, a few there were who died
Of cold and hunger; side by side,
A mother and her infant child
Perished from the blast so wild;
While the father went to seek
Food and fuel, for the weak
And loved ones he had left at home;
So far and long he had to roam,
That, deterred, he came too late
To save them from their unhappy fate.

Like all things else, the snow at last was gone,
The warmer days of February come,
And glad were they to see the earth once more,
Though burned and blackened as before.
Very late it was before the green
Of the fire-dried prairie could be seen.
For a while the vegetation grew,
Then came the drought, and filled
Anew with dread the sinking hearts of those
Who hoped their hardships at a close.


## THE DROUGHT.

The sun beat hot upon the withered grass,
That crackled under foot like molten glass;
And there was heard
No note or call of bird;
Instead of cooling zephyrs' breath,
The southwest simoon brought but death.

Instead of gentle showers, there,
A white heat on the earth did glare,
And vegetation, brown and bare,
Brought forth no food
For man, or beast, or bird;
And all about was heard
A cry of desolation.

The streams were dry.
Above, the clear and pitiless sky
Shone, steady and bright,
From its dazzling height.
The birds had fled —
The fish were dead.
Each morning, filled with dread,
Unrested from the night,
The inhabitants awoke and fed
Upon their scanty bread,
And watched, with longing eyes
And vain expectancy, the skies;
And fain would stand
Watching a cloud no larger than the prophet's
    hand;
But not with equal faith that it would bring
From the dry heavens the longed-for rain.

Sometimes, gigantic size the clouds attained,
Yet all their life-giving bulk retained,
Till far beyond our burning sand,
They reached a happier-fated land,
And there unburdened, in kissing showers,
Upon ladened fields, and fruit and flowers.

Beautiful lakes, in mirage, oft were seen,
In tantalizing vision; and the green
Of tall trees growing close beside,
And cities mirrored in fictitious tide;
Making the people feel like they were stranded
Upon Sahara's desert, empty handed.

Oh, would it never rain!
And ease the burning pain
Of the scorched earth,
And quench this awful dearth!
Would there never again come dew,
Fainting nature to renew!


Must they abandon their prairie home,
For the antelope and buffalo again to roam,
Owners of all.   They had thought it grand,
This smoothly-lying prairie land,
And had planned what beautiful homes  they'd
    make,
And how much comfort and ease they would
    take.


Now, the bustle and stir of ambition all hushed,
Through the quiet and desolation rushed
Visions of once happy homes;
And ever and again there comes,
To overstrained and weary heart,
The longing to return; and so depart


Many, to their former home —
Glad to be gone — yet leaving some,
Who could not go,
To suffer, slow
And bitter pangs of hard privation,
Amounting almost to starvation.

But they struggled bravely on,
Conquering hardships, one by one,
Until, inured to suffering and want,
Nothing could their spirits daunt.

## THE RAIN.

AFTER months of weary waiting—
  Months of heartache and of anguish—
Months of hoping and of praying
  That all nature might not languish,
Came the blessed rain, in torrents,
  Kissing the parched earth, and cooling.
All the moisture held in durance
  For those long months, seemed outpouring—

On the fields and plains so arid,
  And the long-expectant people;
On the dry and dusty high road,
  Came the blessed rain, so needful;
Filling full the creeks and rivers,
  And the little streamlets glad'ning;
Filling full the gaping fissures
  In the dry earth, open standing.

Soon again the grass was green,
  Soon were heard the sweet birds singing;
Here and there, there soon were seen
  Ploughmen with glad hearts returning:

Once again the fine, rich soil,
　　Moistened by refreshing showers,
Yields its fruitage unto toil;
　　And the prairies blaze with flowers.

With thankful hearts and steady hand,
　　People began to improve their homes;
Determined again to reclaim the land
　　From the wild herd which upon it roams.
Cottages neat, and pastures wide,
　　Flowering gardens and stone walls grand,
Young orchards and fields on every side,
　　Pictures of comfort and thrift, now stand.


## THE WALNUT CREEK.

AND, like a bright and happy dream,
The beautiful, winding Walnut stream
　　　　Flows swiftly along,
　　　　With its rippling song,
Where the sumac bright, and willows green,
Bend low to the water's silvery sheen.

Along its valley, green and wide,
Graze flocks and herds on every side;
And at eventide
　　　　The milkmaid's song
　　　　Is wafted along
On the perfumed air, and the quail's "bob-white"—
Scenes of beauty, and sounds of delight.

The herdsman whistles contented and slow,
As homeward he hies, in the sunset glow;
    The lowing of cows,
    As they slowly browse
Along the way home, and the bleating of sheep,
All lend a charm and rythm deep

To the happy and peaceful scene;
Where a feeling of *hominess*, serene,
    Pervades the air
    So soft and fair.
Life in its simplest, happiest mood,
Is life indeed, if understood.


    Softly the wind is blowing —
    Gently my muse is rowing
      In calmer, smoother seas;
    Neither caring nor knowing
    Whither she is going;
      Fanned by the gentle breeze,
      Sweet, as from tropic trees.
    4

## AUGUST.

THE summer's almost done!
And, one by one,
The crops are gathered
In the August sun.
The stack yard is complete;
Beautiful, and replete
With long ricks—brown and yellow—
Of hay and grain so sweet.

The melons are ripening,
The pumpkins are yellowing,
The fruit is mellowing
In the golden sun;
The corn slowly hardening
Within its thick covering—
Nature preparing
For frosts soon to come.

The cricket is singing,
The earth is ringing
With insects creaking
In great delight.
The air is luscious
With fragrance delicious
Of new-mown hay;
There are hints, suspicious,
Of autumn, in the shorter day,

And clear, cool night,
Made glad by the chorus
Beneath us and o'er us —
Tsip, tsip, tsip, tsee–e–e–e–e,
Te–reat, te–reat, te–re–e–e–e.

With repose and restfulness,
Peace and thankfulness —
After days of usefulness —
All nature seems imbued.
The soft and mellow sunshine,
And the cool fresh air, combine
Within us to enshrine
A feeling of joy, subdued.

## THE MEADOW LARK.

O HAPPY and free,
And full of glee,
Is thy song to me,
    Sweet meadow lark!
As, along the way,
Thy cheerful lay,
Like a sound of May,
    Doth cheer the heart!

Always the same,
Great is thy fame,
And blest thy name,
    Sweet meadow lark!

Thy glad note teems
With joy, and seems
Part of the sun's bright beams,
  Sweet meadow lark!


Thy sole ambition,
And intuition,
Seem, to fill the mission
  Of glad'ning the earth!
O that we, too,
All this life through,
Might help to woo
  Some sad heart to mirth!


## THE MIST.

How beautiful, at daybreak,
  To see the mist arise —
Roll itself up like a curtain
  Bordering the skies.


And sometimes, when it's forgotten
  To roll itself up in time,
The sunshine, catching it lingering,
  Glistens each particle fine —

Filling the air with gold dust,
　　And a glory most sublime;
Repaid is he who beholds it
　　For getting up in time.

The birds are gaily twittering
　　Their welcome to the sun;
The chickens lustily heralding
　　That the day is begun.

How narrow seems the horizon,
　　Encircled by the cloud
Of mist, rolled back so perfectly,
　　Which does our view enshroud.

But the sun will soon dispel it,
　　As for centuries it has done,
Flooding the earth with his glory,
　　Widening our horizon.

## OLD-FASHIONED FLOWERS.

MORNING-GLORIES, purple, red, white, and blue —
Flowering beauties of every hue!
Each morning they greet me, cheerful and bright,
Each day giving my heart new delight.

Entwined in their tendrils, the gay Marigold,
It dark red and yellow, flaunting and bold,
Blooms cheerily on, though the splendor of morn-
 ing
Vanishes quickly — evanescent adorning.

Close by, in colors radiant,
A bed of Four-o'clocks, redolent,
Its fragrance sheds on the morning,
Picture of beauty, choice and rare!

Old-fashioned flowers, rare and sweet,
Gaily blooming in quiet retreat!
Dew on the grass — birds in the air —
Beauty and fragrance everywhere!

## THE CAMP-FIRE AT NESS CITY.
### SEPTEMBER 16, 1885.

Not like this, twenty years ago,
 The camp-fire bright,
Amid friends, and peace and plenty
 Shed its light —
But on the tented field,
 To tired and hungry men,
'Twas made to yield
 Some little comfort.

Gloomily, in an enemy's land,
  Its flickering rays shine round;
While, upon every hand,
  The accoutrements of war are found,
And tired soldiers stand,
  Or lie upon the hard ground.


I can see them now,
  After a long and weary march,
Through drizzling rain and snow,
  Under the heaven's leaden arch,
Wearily pitching their tents;
  Each striving hard to go
Beyond his comrade in brave endurance.


Tired, hungry and cold,
In the drear November night,
Visions of home unfold
To the weary soldier's sight:
Thoughts of the cheerful home-light,
The warm supper and the love-light
In loving eyes so bright,
Make the soldier, bold,          •
Weak as a child:
As he notes the dreariness,
And eats his hardened fare,—
Drinks his strong black coffee,
And wishes he were there;
And then, in weariness,
Throws himself on the ground to sleep
And dream of loved ones fair;

While they their vigils keep,
In off'ering prayer
That God their soldier spare.

Yet, sometimes, steadier shone the light
Around a camp-fire blazing bright;
And cheerful men whistled or sang —
With joyful note the camp ground rang;
Good news from home, or new-found hope
That soon the war would close, awoke
Their almost fainting hearts; and then,
Their loved homes they would see again.

At length, the last hard battle fought,
The nation freed — God's purpose wrought —
Each one homeward took his way,
Proud that the right at last had sway.
Home to love and friends again,
He counted not his hardships vain;
But all the brighter burned the flame
Upon the altar fire of home.

All honor to our soldiers brave,
Who risked their health and lives to save
Our country's name
From treason's shame!
And, as around this camp-fire meet
Comrades, who gladly each other greet,
Give a tear and a memory sweet
To those who life itself did yield
Upon a well-fought battle field.

## THE LITTLE SOD HOUSE.

THE little sod house thatched with willows,
  Hanging like yellow-green fringe!
The soft, thick grass for a matting,
  Doth against the fine Brussels impinge.

The walls, it is true, are ungainly,
  But then there is comfort within;
The fire shines as bright, burns as warmly,
  As in palace, or cottage, or inn.

It's deep window seats bright with flowers,
  That fragrance and beauty out cast;
O, many the glad, happy hours
  That within its black walls have been passed!

In the earth, on the earth, of the earth!
  Near nature's great heart are we,
When we gather around the hearth
  Of the sod house, on the prairie sea.

5

## COMPENSATION.

THERE is compensation for every ill,
For all the privations that seem to fill
        Our cup to the brim;
If we are patient, and wait long enough,
Though the way seem rugged, weary and rough,
        It will surely come.

To the dweller on dry and dusty plain
Come visions of trees and golden grain,
        Sweet flowers and fruit.
The image, by contrast, intensifies
The picture dear to us; and verifies
        The truth I bruit.

Terraced gardens and ivy-green walls,
Ruined castles and great waterfalls,
        In fancy, are ours.
We stand 'neath the shade of great branching
    elms,
Or by the cool waters of clear-flowing streams,
        'Mid fanciful bowers.

The poor man, who toils for his daily bread,
In a cottage resting his weary head,
        Rests sweetly there;
Nor envies the rich man his feverish hours,
As he dreams of mortgages, deeds and dowers,
        And life's fitful care.

- The mourner, grieving for her loved ones lost,
Upon a sea of sorrow tempest tossed,
    Seems almost hopeless;
Yet the waves of trouble cease to flow,
Higher than hope; and she's brought to know
    And love the helpless.

To those who, in exile, far from home
And well-known friends, are obliged to roam,
    Friends become dearer;
The dearth of companionship, the heart so needs,
Makes one live in the books he reads,
    And therefore grow wiser.

So with all grades of human life;
There is, for all its weary strife,
    Some compensation—
Some bright spots through the riven cloud—
Some extra-sense with which endowed—
    Sweet consolation!


## PRESENTIMENT.

Ah! why do teardrops start unbidden,
    And long-drawn sighs the bosom heave,
As if by some great sorrow riven,
    And hope had forever taken leave.

The heart seems filled with boding ill —
   With pity for itself congealed;
Like some great harm or sudden chill
   Had come, and all love's fountains sealed.

O then it is, with sudden burst
   Of realty, there dawns upon
Our minds the thought, that e'en the worst
   That happens ere our life be run,

Cannot outlast the great Beyond,
   Where love shall not be filled with care,
And where our lives shall not be stunned
   By storms and withering despair.

## STORM.

O FIERCE storm king, stay thy hand!
Blight not this our beauteous land
With thy desolating breath —
Bringing naught but ice and death;
Gloat not o'er our helplessness —
Thou art conquer'r, we the vanquished;
Stay thy hand, whose ruthlessness,
Long has joy and beauty banished!

Fierce thy reign, and unrelenting —
Nor by pain nor anguish softened;
O'er our prairies, unrepenting,
Thou hast man and beast encoffined,

In mounds of thy fierce, crystalled wrath;
Stalking through these plains, unchallenged,
Naught to intercept thy path:
Surely thou art well avenged
For all the joy, or warmth, or gladness,
Earth or mortal dared to feel,
When by south winds moved from sadness,
And from tempests that congeal
All the pulsing heart of nature,
Setting there its icy seal.
Thou, with all a north king's *hauteur,*
Makest us thy power feel,
And to pray for thy departure—
Cold, thy biting blades, as steel.


Though thou givest us naught of pleasure,
In thy fierce and wild career,
Spare, oh spare, our best-loved treasure—
The lives of friends we hold so dear!
Blight them not by thy cold kisses—
Woo them not with moaning wind;
Fold them not in thy embraces,
Leaving e'en no trace behind!
We can win no promise from thee—
Thou dost fill the heart with dread,
Lest, e'en now, thy cruelty
Takest some we love as dead!


Pity! O our hearts are rended
By this tempest, long unended!

God of the winds, of wave, and sea,
Speak, oh speak, and comfort me!
From Thy throne above, on high,
Let Thy tender, loving eye
Rest on us poor, tempest-tossed
Pilgrims on life's sea embossed;
Let Thy gentle, loving voice
Speak the word that rules all choice
Of wind or storm, and quiets them;
So our frail barks may ever stem
Both physical and mental storms,
That cross our path in countless swarms,
Filling the soul with dread alarm,
Lest those we love may come to harm!
And when, of storms we've faced the last—
Life's dangerous voyage safely past—
O then, at last, most peacefully,
Bring us all to heaven and Thee!


## SUNSHINE.
### JANUARY 19, 1886.

ONCE more we hail the sunshine!
    The tempest at last is passed;
After weeks of weary waiting,
    The light has come at last.

Earth revels in the sunbeams
    Which warm her frozen cheek—
Kissing the icy teardrops,
    And wooing her to speak.

Our hearts, too, ope with gladness
    To let the sunlight in,
For lone, and dark, and gloomy
    These stormy days have been —

Filled full of apprehension,
    For the suffering of those
Who may, from cold and hunger,
    Die in these fearful snows;

Or those compelled by pressure
    Of things of life and death
To face the dreaded current —
    The storm king's icy breath.

But now, at last, 'tis over,
    And all breathe free once more;
Whatever harm is wrought,
    The sun shines as before.

## A THAW.

No longer are our windows frosted o'er
With pleasant pictures, delicate and hoar,
Of ferns and flowers of the summer time,
And diamond crystals wrought in jeweled rime
By skillful artist, through the long night-time;
And now we view the outer world again,
And watch the goings of our fellow-men,
Who have, like us, been housed in winter den,

But now, no longer snow-bound, go abroad,
As is their custom — like the ground-hog, thawed
From out his winter quarters, being wooed
By spring-like breezes — out in search of food;
Right gladly, too, they once again exhume
Themselves, their wonted business to resume.


The great white banks, so lately frozen hard,
Are treacherous now — and here and there the
    sward
Is bare once more. The distant hills loom high,
In outline black and white, against the sky;
And on the moistened breezes sounds traverse
Great distances with ease. One hears the terse
"Whoa" — as the neighboring farmer checks his
    steed,
That long restrained, would gladly try his speed;
A murmur, indistinct, comes from the town;
And bark of dogs that chase the rabbit down;
And joyously and clear, from far and near,
The lusty crowing of the chanticleer;
The children, long kept indoors by the cold,
Now fill the air with cheerful shouts, and mold
The melting snow in forms; the distant lowing
Of cattle impatient for their evening meal;
Or to her calf the mother-cow's soft mooing;
The rattle of the wagon's heavy wheel.
These sounds — a sense of quickened life bestow-
    ing —
Borne on the glad, moist air, upon us steal;

Commingled, too, with many a laughing peal,
Like so many tokens of all human weal.


## TO ———.

Your's the first eyes my little songs did meet;
Your words of praise and appreciation sweet
The first my eager, anxious ears did greet,
As I waited in my quiet country-seat.
As the years pass by, like wingèd horses fleet,
May they all good things bring you, and complete
The measure of your lives with blessings meet.
And when at last, like time, you too have passed
Beyond life's care and work, may there be cast
A glittering crown upon your heads at last.
Accept, kind friends, for your generous praise,
My warmest thanks.  My ambition it did raise
To hope I yet may walk Promethean ways,
And comfort mortals by my simple lays.


## A WINDY DAY.

"'Blow,' did you say?  Now you're mighty
    right!"
And the farmer pulls his hat on tight,
As he struggles hard to unload the hay
He had promised and brought to town to-day.

6

And, "O dear me! what a dreadful plight
My bangs are in!" says the beauty bright,
As she looks in the glass, like a laughing sprite,
And declares that she "Never saw such a fright."

"There, now, goes my blue umberellar!"
And, watching it, the old lady falls down a cellar.
It keeps bravely on till it strikes a poor "feller"
Hard in the face; and he'd like to tell her,
In accents not mild, "To keep her umbrella,
Next time, at home when the wind does blow;
For 'tisn't fair for umbrellas to go
Sailing along through the streets so."

"Heigh-ho, my hat!" and the dignified,
Portly man, with a rapid stride,
Seeks to follow—but woe betide
His dignity; for, side by side,
He and the hat together roll
Over and over, toward the north pole;
He seeking to catch it at every stretch,
But a new gust of wind takes it out of his reach.
Breathless and angry he gives up the chase,
For with such a wind he can never keep pace.
Other hats have a lop-eared expression that's
    droll;
As if, of a sudden, they'd lost all control
Of themselves; and their owners look a sight to
    condole;
Just like some misfortune had happened their
    soul,

Or stocks had gone down of a sudden, and broke
The wheels of their business up, spoke by spoke.
Coat tails assert themselves, standing out
    straight—
Whether old-fashioned, or new cut and late—
Surely things are in a very mixed state.


A housewife is battling with clothes on the line,
While still in the suds I've had to keep mine.
Late home to dinner, you'll find a cross mate,
For nerves will succumb, at last, to such fate.
Papers and boxes fly helter and skelter,
While doors and windows keep up such a clatter
One grows cross, and yet wonders what is the
    matter.



## THE LOST "NARRATIVE."

TO——.

LETTERS I've written, long and short—
Letters of love and of retort;
Letters of friendship, and all sort;
Letters to South and letters to Nort;
Letters to East and letters to West—
But never, no never, 'mong all the rest,
Was accused of giving, to those I love best—
Not even to those I called but friend—
That part of my time you call the "tail-end."

Time flies! and, like Tam O'Shanter's mare,
Is tailless long ere one's aware,
Or reaches the running water, where
The witches of hurry and of care
Cease annoying us, and stare;
And there is only left us, there,
The bare escape; while, everywhere,
Duties unpleasant and duties fair,
Burdens heavy and hard to bear,
Others pleasing and light as air,
Crowd, unfinished, plucking Time's hair;
Till we, in utter and blank despair,
Wonder if ever, or anywhere,
Before was seen such a tailless mare
As the flying steed, so bald and bare,
Which the penniless writer rides with care.


So accuse me not of giving to you
The *narrative* to which I've lost all clue:
I've plucked from Time's forelock some moments
    new —
In which I could write some sentiments true;
Though poorly expressed, I hope that a few
May revive my true image, in your heart, anew.
That blessings on earth and in heaven accrue
To your share, is the wish of—adieu.

# EDDIES OF MEMORY.

"How long we live, not years, but actions, tell."
*—Heath.*
"That man lives twice who lives the first life well."
*—Tennyson.*

## THE POET'S DESTINY.

'TIS the poet's *forte* to cheer;
And only in this sphere,
Is his life at all in gear:

To make men nobler, better;
And thus fulfill the letter
Of genius, without fetter:

To make men braver, truer;
And fit them to endure
Temptations which allure.

The earth, the air, and sky,
All, are lessons, if we try
To understand, as we go by:

Lessons which will work as leaven,
While by earth storms we are driven —
Leading upward unto heaven.

Beauty on the mountain steep —
Beauty in the fountain deep —
Beauty from the stars doth peep.

'Tis the poet's pleasant task
All their beauties to unmask,
And in bold, clear light to bask;

Leading with him, by his zeal,
All the nations; and to heal
Many, from despair's dark seal.


## LIFE.

O LIFE! how bitter-sweet thou art!
  What a shaded picture!
  What a strange admixture
Does ebb and flow within each heart!

What restless longing after pleasure,
  That ever eludes our grasp:
  How harshly, on our natures, rasp
Our many sad and grievous failures!

For disappointments sear the soul,
  And callous all our nature,
  Till, in each distorted feature,
Life seems a rag-a-tattered scroll

That's hardly worth unrolling,
Unless we look beyond ourselves
To worthier object than ourselves —
Joy thus unfolding.

The selfish heart knows little bliss;
For if, for its own pleasure,
And life of idle leisure,
It lives — bliss is not gained like this.

If, from the bitter, some sweet one would gain,
He must strive for the good of others,
As if all men were his brothers,
And, in this way, lasting joy attain.

He must soothe the ever-maddening pain —
The restless, fevered longing,
Through so many hearts now thronging —
Of the anxious, overburdened brain;

Must help the poor or nurse the suffering;
Teach the rich how best to use
Their wealth; and thus infuse
Into each life desires ennobling.

In this way, surely, may be brought,
Out of life's bitter, the sweet —
Some pleasures which are meet,
To make life glad, and worth the thought.

## A VOICE.

Once I dreamed of flying,
And a voice kept crying,
Without cease or tiring,
  "Higher, higher, higher!"

Yes, higher, higher,
We should aspire,
Till gleams the fire
  From the golden gate;

And the angels song,
From the white-robed throng,
Is wafted along
  To our raptured state.

And nevermore,
On that shining shore,
Will we deplore
  The effort we make.


## THE DEAR OLD HYMN.

One of the sweetest memories, mother, dear,
  Of all my childhood days—
  Pure as the moon's soft rays,
  While traveling weary ways,
Is of seeing you sit sewing, near

The window; while, in voice so clear,
And low, and sweet, you sang the dear,
Familiar hymn you loved so well.
I can find no words to tell
The thoughts that in my bosom swell,
When, far away from thee, I hear
The same old hymn, to me so dear.

"O Thou Fount of ev'ry blessing"—
 Is the soft refrain;
 I can sing no further,
 For tears that fall like rain;
 For, thronging, comes a train
 Of thoughts that are both pain
 And pleasure.

"Never let me wander from Thee"—
 I try to sing,
 But cannot bring
 The words to utterance:
So oft I've wandered, and so far—
So far from thee, my guiding star—
My gentle mother! who, with care,
Did guide and shield from ev'ry snare;
And from whose lips, so oft, I've heard
The low, sweet song of—"By Thy Word
And Spirit guide me." And I long,
Again, to hear you sing that song.

Thou wert more than mother to me—
Sweet companion, sister, friend!

7

And to all my girlish fancy
A sympathetic ear did lend.
And thy gentle hands enrobed me
For my baptism, and my bridal day.
And twice, when death almost did lay
His icy hand upon me, 'twas thou
Who nursed me back to life again;
And, from my earliest memory,
Thou hast lovingly forged the golden chain
Which binds me close to thee.   Our love
Is eternal!   "Father, guide us, then,
Till we reach Thy courts above."


## CONTENTMENT.

O BLEST content,
    I woo, I covet thee!
What charm is lent
    By thy sweet mystery,
        To banish care!

What peace and joy
    Thou bringest us! Pure gold,
Without alloy,
    And pleasures manifold,
        Thou art to all!

Spirit, sweet and rare,
    Thy help we invocate,

Make life seem fair!
  Our natures renovate,
    Our discontent!


## TO MARIA AND MARY H. M———.

O THOSE glad and happy days of childhood,
  When, free from toil and care,
We wandered in the quiet wildwood,
  Or strayed in fields so fair;

Gathering the early, fragrant spring flowers;
  Swinging in the grape-vine swing;
Seeking the cosiest, shadiest bowers;
  Listening to the brown thrush sing!

Never so sweet have been the flowers
  From green-house or garden rare,
As those we gathered after showers —
  Spring-beauties and blue-bells fair.

And oft we wished our hands were larger,
  That more we might carry home;
While already every vase and pitcher,
  Was like a flowery dome.

Do you remember how we could hear
  The voice of old Cooper's Falls,
Roaring and rushing, in the spring of the year,
  Over its rocky walls?

Later, in the golden, autumn sun,
    The brown hazel nuts we'd gather
Along the pasture fence, which run
    West from the village border.

And after the frost, the walnuts, dun,
    Were added to our measure;
With housewifely instinct we would sum
    Up all our winter treasure.

And then, when the village school began,
    We brought the same glad zest
Into our studies, with which we ran
    Upon the nutting quest.

At recess, we'd play at "Hide and seek,"
    Or "Blackman's" boisterous game;
With quickened pulses and rosy cheek,
    Our "base" we would regain.

What glowing pictures we made, so fine,
    Of what we'd have when grown;
And sometimes we'd draw, in bold outline,
    A palace for our home.

Ah! dainty, dreamy little maidens!
    How little did we know
Of all in life that clogs and saddens—
    Of its vain pomp and show.

How few, of our many air castles,
 We ever realized!
And cottages, more than castles,
 In after years we prized.

But if we could bring the earnestness
 To bear upon life's care,
We gave to our childish playfulness,
 'Twould all of it outwear.

## GRANT.

Grant, our loved hero, *dead!*
With bated breath, we read,
And then, with softer tread,
 Pursued our daily care.
The silent man of deed,
Who knew his country's need,
At last, from suffering freed,
 Rests from all earthly care.

O noble spirit, rare!
What joy in the realms of the air,
At the accession, fair,
 Of thy dear company.
Great among men thou wert,
And great shall be thy part
In the deep fountain heart
 Of the angelic symphony.

Thou wert our nation's pride!
All over land and tide,
Honor, on every side,
　　And love, awaited thee:
For was it not to thee
We owed our liberty?
Our nation's unity,
　　To thy great utility?

The power of his life,
With noble deeds so rife,
In all the scenes of strife
　　Through which he bravely passed,
Is felt by every one;
And he, his journey run,
Bearing life's scorching sun,
　　Useful to the last.

## COMMENCEMENT AT O——A.

It is eighteen years
Since the hopes and fears,
Of my last commencement day;
　Yet I seem again
　To breathe, as then,
The sweet June roses gay;

　As their fragrance sweet
　All our senses greet,
In delicious intoxication;

And wafted along,
Through the joyous throng,
Are the voices of friends and relation.

Wreaths and flowers
Entwine, like bowers,
Each column and window high;
And in each breast
Is the anxious zest
Of a great occasion nigh.

How fearful we feel
Lest we should fail
To meet our friends' expectation;
And when, at last,
Our effort passed,
How sweet their commendation.

The conqueror great,
Or man of state,
Ne'er felt the exultation;
And ne'er attained
The bliss we gained,
From friends' appreciation.

And then we pressed
Hands we loved best,
In silent anguish parting;
One going here,
Another there—
Each to his life work starting.

I should like to know,
As old they grow,
What each one's fate has been;
And whether, or not,
The true life-thought
Of each has been wrought in;

And whether, at last,
When life's school is past,
We shall hear our Father say:
"Well done! Well done!
Thou hast laurels won!"
At the great commencement day.


## TO CLARA B——.

DEAR CLARA: We cannot see why, all at once,
    Thou should'st be so bereft;
Of all thy loved and cherished ones,
    So very few are left.

I knew thee when a blue-eyed child,
    Happy and free as a bird;
As a maiden, gentle voiced and mild,
    Thy ringing laugh oft heard.

First was taken thy gentle sister—
    Pure as a lily white;
And though you mourned, and sadly missed her,
    This first grief was but light,

Compared to those thou hast endured;
　For then, thy tender mother,
In the midst of her own grief, soothed and cured
　The grief of every other.


How much she was beloved by all!
　Possessed of the rare gift
Of helping up the weak, who fall—
　The saddened to uplift!


Patient, pure, loving, and kind!
　A truly noble type
Of a thoughtful, gentle, womanly mind,
　By Christian faith made ripe.


But just when most her company you prized,
　And her sweet counsel sought,
She, too, was taken; and you realized
　The pain that loving brought.


And then, ere many months had passed,
　Father, brother, and child
Were summoned—and you felt the icy blast
　Of grief, stormy and wild.　　　　　　'


No loving mother, then, to soothe
　Thy bitter, sobbing grief!
No father this rough path to smooth!
　Nor yet the sweet relief

8

Of little hands at thy sad heart,
   To woo thee to forget
Thy sore bereavements, and to start
   A hope to live for yet!

Yes, surely, sad has been thy lot,
   And sore thy chastening;
Thou couldst not have borne it all, hadst not
   Thou sought God's strengthening.

As, out of the rude block of stone,
   Thy skillful fingers bring
Beauty and form, from these alone,
   By cutting and chiseling —

So the Great Artist shapes our lives,
   "Rough-hewing" to His will,
Till fit our souls for heaven's archives;
   Then He'll bid us, "Peace! be still."


## ✗ PATER, SALUTAMUS!
### JUNE 6, 1885.

JUST sixty years have passed away,
Since first beheld the light of day
   Our father dear.
How lightly time has touched his brow!
How little wrinkled, even now,
   His placid feature!

Yet life to him has been no play,
But full of endeavor to allay
   His fellows' pain.
For this he's toiled early and late;
For this, indifferent to fate
   And worldly gain.

How many, many will bless thy skill?
Thy lion heart, thy rousing will,
   Which nobly fought
The fell disease, the racking pain!
New modes of healing to attain
   He's ever sought.

Though not in this alone we're blest:
Nature gave him a rich bequest—
   A heart with treasure fraught.
Though large the place assigned his art,
Each of us feels we have a part
   In his life thought.

Wife, children, children's children, all,
The old and young, the large and small,
   Receive his tender care.
Noble, generous, gifted!  Proud
Are we to love and honor thee!  Endowed
   With gifts most rare.

Thou, too, wert blest; for by thy side
Has closely walked, whate'er betide,
   So mild and kind,

Our gentle mother; ever near,
To help, inspire, comfort and cheer
    Thy burdened mind.

May years be given thee on earth;
May cheery friends around thy hearth
    Make glad thy soul;
And when our Father calls thee home,
May we, too, hear the welcome "Come!"
    And reach the goal.

We gather round this board, to-day,
With happy hearts that we can say
    We are all here—
Father, mother, sister, brother;
With joy, again we greet each other,
    From far and near.

Each brings some token of his love—
Each tries his high esteem to prove;
    And, with the rest,
Accept this tribute from the pen
    Of your Celeste. —


## THE SABBATH.

Sweet Sabbath morn! how bright thou dawnest—
    Night's curtain furled!
What comfort, peace, and rest, thou bringest
    The tired world!

Sweet Sabbath bells ring out for joy,
  In pleasant chimes;
Their joyous peals bring thoughts, to enjoy,
  Of olden times:

When with sweet, old-fashioned roses
  Entwined in hat and hair,
A little girl's hand reposes
  In that of her father dear,
    As they walk to the village church.

The day is radiant and bright,
  The air with fragrance ladened;
The sun gives a steadier light—
  Nature's great heart is burdened
    With joy it throbs to express,

Yet keeps its glories subdued,
  This calm, sweet day of rest;
Earth, air and sky seem imbued
  With reverence, and blest
    With brightness and repose.

Who of us does not remember
  Many such Sabbaths as this?
Our young hearts, receptive and tender;
  When life itself seemed bliss—
    Our hope so strong and bright.

Years have dulled the brightness
  Of this world's plans and hopes,

And taken somewhat of the lightness
  From our hearts—as down life's slopes
We slowly, surely tread.

But, to all our cares and fears,
  Comes the sweet Sabbath rest;
With its surcease from toil, it rears
  Strength in our tired breast.
  God grant us rest at last!


## NOBODY REALLY CARES.

Is life so cold and selfish,
  So full of cynic bears?
Is human nature elfish,
  That nobody really cares
If our hearts are slowly breaking,
  And unanswered are our prayers?

Is there no true heart, loving,
  That kindly our sorrows shares?
No proffered help, thus proving
  That somebody really cares?
Then dark, indeed, is our pathway;
  Despair comes unawares!

Has no one learned the lesson,
  In all this wide world through,
Christ taught—"To love each other,
  As I have lovèd you?"

Ah! this would soothe our anguish,
  And our heart's strength renew.

Is there not within ourselves,
  Some throb of tenderness,
Which many times impels
  To deeds of generousness?
Do we not really care
  If a friend is in distress?

Then rid yourself of the thought,
  "Nobody really cares;"
Love's choicest gifts are brought
  To him who nobly bears
The ill as well as good of life —
  And somebody really cares.


## TO ESTHER ——.

### A SONNET.

TRULY noble and rare
  Is thy gentle care,
  And life of sacrifice
For father and brothers dear.
Thy goodness, like a surplice,
  Is thrown around all;
Thy good deeds, like an orison
Or benediction, fall
Upon all who are near.
Wide is thy horizon,

When a field of good thou seekest;
Unto the poor and suffering
A helping hand thou reachest;
But brightest, thy home offering.


## EPITHALAMIUM.

UPON THE DOUBLE WEDDING OF JENNIE AND MAMIE F——.

GOOD luck! good luck, all this life through,
To those who, under the magic horse-shoe—
    With its "power to charm
    Away all harm"—
    Stood arm in arm!
May their lives be fair
As the blonde's fair hair,
Deep and rich as the brunette's eyes;
    Gay as each guest,
    And full of zest;
Pure as the azure blue skies.
Happy their home—
May they never roam
Away from kindred and friends;
    May peace surround,
    And love abound,
May every charm which lends
    Lustre and beauty,
    Unto life's duty,
In the sweet home-life be theirs:
    Patience and gentleness,
    Wisdom and holiness,

Guiding them safely through cares;
  And when, at last,
  Life's safely past,
And eternity breaks on the soul,
  Enjoy evermore,
  On the beautiful shore,
Love, home, and heaven, their goal.


## THE POET'S CONFUSION.

WHERE are all the fancies
  That sometimes come unbidden?
Now I would summon them,
  They all have gone and hidden.

Neither plan nor harmony
  Has my mind—but, void
Of all shape and symmetry,
  Imagination toyed,

Idly, with this and that;
  Darting here and yonder,
Like a butterfly at play,
  With time and sweets to squander.

O come, my Muse, do not
  Play hide-and-seek with me!
And I'll all things else forsake,
  And meekly follow thee

9

Whithersoc'er thou leadest—
· To the realms of fancy fair,
To the highest mountain air,
    Or the depths of dark despair:

Only lead thou steadily,
    Boldly and unflinchingly,
And I'll be thy true disciple
    Most willingly!


## COW BELLS.

### INSCRIBED TO J. H. B.

ONE sound, more than all others,
    Touches memory's bell,
Bringing thoughts of sweet-brier and clovers,
    Violets and asphodel:

The slow ting-ling of the cow bells
    Brings pictures of flowery meads;
Visions of lanes and shady dells,
    Cool streams and flowing reeds.

As I sit in my home on the prairie,
    With half-closed eyes, and hear
The measured sound, and cheery,
    It brings the past so near:

A child again, I wander
    Through green and shady nook,
Or through the briers clamber,
    Along the rippling brook,

Hunting berries and fishing,
 With bucket, bait, and hook;
Under the tall tress resting —
 Reading our choicest book;


While, now and then, the stillness
 Is broken by the sound
Of tinkling bells in the distance —
 Then quiet all around.


And occasionally the plashing
 Of some bird or twig, apart,
In the cool water dropping.
 Causes one to start.


As later, we homeward go,
 At nearly the close of day,
The cows, soft eyed and slow,
 We drive o'er the woodland way,


Through long lanes, green and shady —
 The western sky aglow;
Mother has supper ready,
 And we are ready, too.


So, now, when I hear the measure,
 The ting-ling, ting-ling slow,
The cows coming home from the pasture,
 Backward my fancies go —

To the pleasant rambles of childhood,
  My brother and I used to gain,
Along the creek in the wildwood —
  Home again through the lane.


## OCTOBER.

Cooler are the days,
  And pleasanter;
Softer the sun's rays,
  And yellower;
No longer the bright blaze,
But a quiet restful haze,
O'er all nature, strays.
  Ripened is the maize,
    And perfected;     .
  The farmers go their ways
    Gathering it;
Bringing the pumpkins yellow,
And the fruit so mellow;
Breaking up the fallow.

Happy autumn days,
  How I love you!
Busy country ways,
  I sing of you!
And on the farm, at night,
Around the fireside bright,
A picture greets the sight:

The father, with his paper,
  Sits reading it;
The daughter, with fingers taper,
  Crocheting mits;
The mother, with her, knitting,
Her loved ones is refitting
For winter's winds so biting.

The son, with slate and pencil,
  Is figuring;
And, fit for an artist's stencil,
  The cat, purring;
Picture of comfort and rest,
In this quiet country nest—
The home we love the best.
  Simplicity and repose
    Such pictures tell;
  No matter how the world goes,
    This part is well:
And while the frost king bold,
In icy clutch, does hold
The family close, behold
What love it doth enfold,
And hardy genius mold!

## A DREAM.

LAST night I had a dream,
In which all things did seem
Arranged to suit my fancy.

I was in some quaint old town,
With many trees; and, walking down
A quiet street,
As if by necromancy,
Beautiful and complete,
A house for princes meet
Did my wondering vision greet.

Its structure was of brick;
Stately its walls, and thick—
Massive and imposing;
Its windows stained,
And, like cathedral's, arching.
Flowers from the tropics,
And the northern spruce,
Fountains clear and sparkling—
All that can conduce
To the pleasure of the optics,
For beauty or utility,
Seemed there retained;
Taste joined to stability.

Sweet music filled the air;
And round it, everywhere,
The spirit of beauty fair
  Seemed hovering.

By some good chance,
  I was then invited
Inside this splendid manse;
  And I was there delighted

To find my husband at my side,
To be my favored guide
Through these grand halls so wide.

The house was furnished, throughout,
  In elegance and taste —
  Intensely rich yet chaste;
Harmonious within as without.
And it was owned, no doubt,
  By some one of high caste.

Each room delighted me;
And I was always shown
The convenience of the place.
The last we went to see
Suited me specially —
As if some one had known
My likings; and its grace
And quiet beauty pleased me.
    "This, if we lived here,
      Should be my very own,"
I said; "for I could not have done
It more to my liking;
Rich it is and striking,
  Yet full of comfort and cheer."

"It is thine own," he said,
"And all around is thine."
  And I, as one who dreamed, or read
  A fairy tale, scarce breathed for dread
  Lest it should vanish. "Mine?
  Whence this princely gift, and fine?"

And while, with wondering eyes,
I gazed in mute surprise,
    My husband laughingly
    Replied, "My gift to thee."
Then, from out ev'ry corner,
Came my friends and former
Neighbors—old Albia friends,
Whose presence to the scene now lends
    Still more enchantment;
They clap their hands in glee,
And laughingly, at me,
Shake their heads—so pleased to see
    My great astonishment.

"Do I wake or am I dreaming?"
    Yet this very pleasant seeming
    Holds me spellbound, with its teeming
    Joy and gladness. Eyes are beaming
    With true love light; mine are streaming
    Now with grateful, happy tears.

   \*      \*      \*      \*      \*      \*

Ah, 'tis all a dream!
Vanished the house so fine,
And the forms divine
Of well beloved friends.
Yet it so real seemed,
I scarce believed I dreamed.

## TO SARAH ELIZABETH A——.
(Princess)     (Consecrated)

### A SONNET.

A PRINCESS, indeed, thou art,
  With yellow hair and hazel eyes;
An impulsive and a loving heart
  That is always ready, and ever tries
To help the needy, and heal the dart
Of sin and sorrow, in every heart.
Consecrated, too, art thou;
  For, to our Father's will,
Thou did'st ever meekly bow
  Thine own heart still.
"A princess consecrated to God"—
  Thy name does suit thee well;
Thy Christian zeal thy friends all laud,
  Thy noble bearing tell.


## MOONLIT CLOUDS.

I LIKE the moonlit clouds,
  With their ever-changing scenes,
Shifting as life's panorama,
  Fitful as its dreams.

As I gaze, alone and enraptured,
  All kinds of shapes they take;
10

Filling the heavens with glory,
   And the beautiful pictures they make.

In the south, a ship is sailing
   Upon a smooth-waved sea;
But, like the ship of our longing,
   'Tis sailing leeward from me.

Another, like a flying steed,
   Is coursing through the air
Like a swift-winged messenger
   To earth, from worlds so fair.

Great steeples, in bold relief—
   Mountains, and sea, and land;
Rich-tinted pictures are they,
   Drawn by the Master Hand.

At length a great black cloud
   Seems to swallow up the moon,
But, like the others, restless,
   Passes away soon.

And I noticed, as I gazed
   Upon the moonlit ray,
It seemed to shine the brighter
   When the cloud had passed away.

And so 'tis with life's troubles,
   Which darken and obscure
Almost the light of reason,
   So hard they are to endure—

When the cloud has passed over the soul,
　And hope shines out once more,
The light seems brighter, steadier,
　And purer than before.


And we are stronger from the strife;
　The soul made free and pure
By the rugged discipline of life —
　And clouds will not long obscure.


## TO LILLIAN A——.

### IN MEMORIAM.

O LILLIAN, so sweet and fair!
　So full of graceful symmetry!
Such beauty thy smooth brow didst wear,
　When last I saw and talked with thee —
I cannot think of thee as dead,
And thy beautiful, proud head
Laid low upon the lea.
Surely "Death loves a shining mark,"
Or he had not found thee;
So fair, so beautiful and young —
Thy life a poem half unsung,
And full of sweetest harmony.
All beautiful things thou didst so treasure —
There may'st thou have them, in full measure!

## ✗ NOTHING "WORTH WHILE."

"It is hard to believe long together that anything is 'worth while,' unless there is some eye to kindle in common with our own, some brief word uttered now and then to imply that what is infinitely precious to us is precious alike to another mind."—*George Eliot.*

THERE is nothing worth while
  Unless shared by another;
What is fortune's sweet smile
  If it glads not our brother?—
It is nothing worth while.

The sweetest of song
  The sirens can sing
Allures us not long,
  Unless we can bring
Our best friend along.

The joy of beholding
  A beauteous picture,
Loses half the unfolding
  Of its soft-tinted feature,
To a lonely heart viewing.

And wisest tales known,
  If they do not beguile
Other hearts than our own,
  Are hardly worth while,
Though in bard's sweetest tone.

The choicest of food,
　To the one who prepares it,
Is not half so good
　If nobody shares it,
And in silence he brood.

What a bauble is fame,
　If there is none
To speak our own name
　As the dearest one!
Ah! life is tame.

So there's nothing worth while,
　If enkindles no eye
With a thought or a smile
　At the same glad sky—
O there's nothing worth while.

'Tis companionship sweet
　The heart most craves;
Love's glances meet,
　And the spirit laves
In a honeyed retreat.


## HOPE.

O RESTLESS, longing heart!
Why do the teardrops start,
　At the sad thought of parting
From all the loved ones dear!
What doubt and anxious fear,

For what the future holds in store; —
Fear lest we shall meet no more,
    In all life's wandering.


If this were all of life,        .
It would be naught but strife,
    And love an idle dream.
All pleasure would be pain,
And worldly losses gain;
All nature incomplete —
Only oblivion sweet —
    And life a stagnant stream:


No light, nor love, nor hope,
In the universe; we'd grope
    In almost total darkness.
Useless 'twould be to strive
For love, or wealth, or dive
Into the mines of knowledge deep;
If death be an eternal sleep,
    This life's too short for gladness.


I'm glad it is not true —
This picture dark I drew
    From sad imaginings.
There is a land most vernal,
Where affection blooms eternal;
Where all our loved ones, fair,
Will meet; and, freed from care,
    Shall cease their wanderings.

## TO FRIENDS AT McPHERSON.

I MUST put away my longing
For those who know and love me,
Stifle the memories, thronging,
Of the past, so pleasant to me,
    And most resolutely
    Face life's present duty,
And make friends of these strangers about
    me.

This was what I said,
When frst I came among you;
    Shrinking away in dread
    From associations new;
But not long till hearts so warm
As yours had penetrated through
The icy mail of cool reserve;
    And, very soon, I knew
    And loved you all. No form
Of language I can use can serve
To show explicitly to you
The love I bear you, kind friends, true.

## THANKSGIVING.

WE truly thank Thee, our Father above,
For the manifold tokens of Thy love,
Which Thou, in mercy, dost bestow
Upon Thy creatures, high and low!

For life itself—a glorious boon,
E'en though its flower vanish soon;
'Tis like a richly-flowing tune,
Or quiet glory of the moon.

For health of body, and of mind,
For dear friends many, true and kind;
For food and raiment, and the light
Of our loved home, this Thanksgiving night.

For country, too, we grateful are;
That peace and plenty are her share;
Nor strife, nor war her glory mar;
Her light shines out, a guiding star.

For all these blessings, we adore
Thy holy name; and still implore
Thy gifts as rich, this coming year;
And may we serve in love, not fear.


## SUNSHINE AND SHADE.

How checkered is this life
    By sunshine bright, and shade!
How full of toil and strife!
    Of joy and pain 'tis made.

With heavy burdens rife,
    And joys the heart to glad;
O ever changeful life,
    Thou art most glad and sad!

Take comfort while thou canst,
　For many ills will come;
The present, thus enhanced,
　May help thee some

The darkest hours to bear,
　When all the sunlight's gone,
And fit thee for the care
　Which comes still further on.

Enjoy then to the fullest
　The pleasures that thou hast!
Be glad for joys the smallest,
　For aye they cannot last!

Yet forget not, in the darkest hour,
　Dense forests have their glade;
The sun, at length, exerts his power,
　And penetrates the shade.

And so it is with life —
　God's penetrating grace,
Through all the toil and strife,
　Will shine to darkest place.


## THE WINDS.

Blow, winds, blow!
How many tales ye know
Of sorrow and of woe,
As defiantly ye blow!

11

How many tales of joy!
As, idly, thou dost toy,
And flaxen curls annoy,
Which love's caress employ.

Blow, moist spring winds, blow!
Increase the streamlet's flow,
And give a ruddy glow
To the cheeks of those who row..

Blow, gentle winds, and low,
So softly now, and slow,
That I can scarcely know
Whence or whither ye go!

Sigh, gentle zephyrs, sigh,
As softly ye pass by
The place wherein doth lie
Our loved and lost ones, nigh!

Moan, ye wild winds, moan
For the summer that has flown —
For the widow's silent groan —
And her loneliness bemoan!

Blow, ye swift winds, blow,
And quickly onward go;
Too many things ye know
Of mortals here below!

# ONE HUNDRED AND THIRTY-SIXTH PSALM.

O GIVE thanks unto the Lord; for He is good:
  For His mercy endureth forever:
Who giveth unto all abundant food,
    And moves all things by His will—a mighty
      lever.

O give thanks unto the mighty Lord of Lords:
  For His mercy endureth forever;
He hath redeemed us from the grievous hordes —
  Our enemies shall trample us, no never.

To Him alone who doeth wonders great:
  Whose mercy endureth forever:
Who remembered us when in our low estate —
  In tender mercy blessed His people ever.

To Him who made the sun to rule by day,
  To give unto His creatures brilliant light;
The moon and stars holds ever in their way,
  To cheer and lighten up the weary night.

To Him who by His wisdom made the heaven;
    And by whose hand so strong, and outstretched
      arm,
The waters of the Red Sea, high, were driven,
    That, through, His people passed and feared no
      harm:

But overthrew King Pharaoh and his host,
  When he to follow Israel did endeavor,
And thought he had o'ertaken them almost,
  The waters high God did no longer sever.


And now His goodness and His love so great,
  His promises do certainly assever,
Are thrown round those of high and low estate:
  For His mercy endureth forever.


## SIXTEENTH WEDDING ANNIVERSARY.

I AM thinking, dear, of our wedding day,
  When life all seemed so bright;
No shadow of care or grief had fallen,
  To cast its withering blight.


O'er fond, fair dreams of the future we dreamed,
  Transcendentally beautiful;
No place in the picture was left for shades,
  For all was light and cheerful.


This world seemed so much like a fairy land,
  With crystal palaces white;
We thought the sun would forever shine,
  And there would be no night.

Bright fancies we wove, and air castles built,
  Of the ideal life we would live;
The home we would have, the things we would
    do;
  Brightest touches to life we would give.


Time passed.  There was much of beauty and
    joy —
  Much of sorrow and care as well;
Our fairy picture had shades in perspective,
  And many an air castle fell.


Our fond ideal gave place to the real;
  Thorns grew in fields Elysian;
Not here, but yonder, we have learned to turn
  Our longing, tear-dimmed vision.


Yet, through all the struggles of many years,
  Love's sun has never set;
Though clouds sometimes obscured the light,
  The days are halcyon yet.


And when we cross o'er to the other shore,
  Then we will realize
The fond, fair dreams we once dreamed here be-
    low,
  In the beauty of the skies.

## THE ORPHAN.

THE night is cold, and dark, and dreary,
  And fierce and wild the wind is blowing.
Without, stands one so sad and weary,
  While, fast and faster, it is snowing.

Within, are comfort and good cheer —
  The ringing laugh of mirth and gladness;
The happy circle gathered here
  Knows naught of wretched want or sadness.

Without, benumbed by winter's blast,
  Alone she stands as if in trance;
And, at the scene within, is cast
  Her burning, hungry, longing glance.

She, too, a happy home had known,
  Like this one full of warmth and pleasure —
Ere death had come, and wealth had flown,
  And left her naught of earthly treasure.

And long she stands and looks within,
  And listens with strained ears to hear
Sweet sounds of music, that have been
  Well known to her, one time, and dear.

Then, shivering, she turns away,
  With bitter thoughts and aching brow;
Her attic seeks, and tries to pray —
  O God of orphans, hear her now!

She prays for faith and strength to see,
    Through all her want and poverty,
God's providence and equity,
    And why life's seeming subtlety.


Who knows what changes time may bring
    To happiest hearts or gayest scene?
For fortune is a fickle thing—
    We cannot count on its gifts, I ween.


O ye who know not want nor care!
    Whose ev'ry wish by love's supplied;
Who live in homes so bright and fair,
    Take pity at this Christmas-tide,
    And scatter gifts afar and wide.


## TIME.

Too swiftly time is flying,
        Ah, me!
And all around me lying,
        Things incomplete I see.


E'en now it is high noontide—
        To me!
Life's morning did so swiftly glide
        Into eternity!

So much I meant to do,
        Undone!
Noon! and night will soon ensue —
        A lifetime quickly run!

Life's sands are measured fast —
        Unerringly;
'Tis scarce begun till past!
        Death claims us willingly!


## A BAYONET CHARGE.

WRITTEN UPON HEARING THE HON. S. R. PETERS DESCRIBE A
CHARGE UPON THE ENEMY'S WORKS.

O, THE dread din of battle!
The thunder of the cannon's roar —
The pools of human gore —
The clatter and the rattle
Of horses hoofs and musketry!

"Charge, bayonets, charge!"
For the enemy's breastworks, charge!
Double-quick, march!"
Rang through the sunlit arch
Of the clear, blue sky above them.

One glance at the sun's bright ray,
And one thought of home, that may
Be the last they can see or give —
For who shall die or live,
Not one of the great throng knows.

Then with bayonets fixed and glistening,
Each to his heart throbs listening,
The solid phalanx goes,
Even to death's last thoes,
Bravely, steadily, unflinchingly.

You can hear the manly shout
Of brave men, who all about
Encounter the jagged lattice
Of the sharp-pointed abbattis,
So hard to overcome.

The cruel shot and shell,
With a spite no tongue can tell,
Hew them down on right and left;
But the places which are cleft
Are quickly filled by others.

Line after line is broken,
And filled e'er command is spoken,
And at last the strong works yield;
But strewn is the grassy field
With those who will never know.

And the men with the flush and glory
Of surely attained victory
Press on, and the battle is gained.
But O, the dead and maimed
Who have paid the dreadful price!

The enemy's forces are scattered—
Their strong works torn and battered;

12

Our flag, from the parapet,
Waves high, ere the sun is set,
And victorious cheers resound.

But after the first glad shout
Of victory has rung out,
There comes a dreadful hush;
To the victors' hearts there rush
Fears for their comrades dear.

For over the fallen they charged—
With fury and speed they had charged!
And, mayhap, their own iron heels,
Had given the wound that seals
The death-doom of their friend.

"Where's John, my dearest comrade,
Whom last I saw press onward
With the courage of Achilles?"
And, down upon his knees,
He seeks him 'mong the dying.

The sun in undisturbed
Quiet and beauty is setting;
While many a hero, unobserved,
Slowly his life blood is letting—
Dying for the land he loves.

Brave, *bravest* of all!
Even death does not appall

The noble soldier's heart;
For he has borne his part
For his loved country's weal.

## SOMETIME.

Some day, sometime, O tired breast,
Above life's storm tossed, billowy crest,
Thou shalt have a long, sweet rest!
And never again know weariness.

The knowledge sought, but unattained,
Shall there so easily be gained;
And ne'er again our hearts be pained
By aspirations sorely maimed.

The songs we cannot sing below
Shall there be given us to know;
And purer than the lilies' blow,
Our garments — whiter than the snow.

Sometime, our wistful eyes shall see
And solve what now is mystery;
Why truth is captive, error free,
And life so full of misery.

And there, at last, our high ideal
Of love and harmony shall be real:
Our brows not wreathed with bitter cerrial,
But love's bright chaplets — crowns imperial.

## FANTASIES.

### I.—REGRET.

Too late in life, my life work has begun;
I feel in breathless haste, lest life be run
Before the half I want to do is done.
So late the dream of childhood is fulfilled—
So late before my heart with rapture thrilled—
Or poetic ecstacy its measure filled
    With overflowing song.

### II.—APPREHENSION.

Sometimes there comes to me a dread
Lest I should lose the shining thread—
    The mystic key,
    Unraveling to me
    The labyrinths of the sea
    Of time, in poesy;—
Fear, lest quickly from my heart,
Just as it came, it may depart.

### III.

Are the gifts of the Muse unstable,
Like the gods of Grecian fable?
Bestowing favors to deceive—
Alluring one, and then take leave?

### IV.—REASSURANCE.

Thou would'st not so wicked be—
Tempting one so fancy free,
And then desert most cruelly!

I'll tune my lyre anew to thee,
And sing thy praise in melody,
And thou wilt then abide with me.

### V.—SONG TO THE MUSE.

Beautiful, art thou, as Helen!
Like Minerva, great and wise!
Working in men's hearts like leaven—
Leading upward to the skies,
By the brightness of thine eyes,
And thy songs of home and heaven.

Thou hast forged a silver chain,
Which binds our hearts to thee for aye;
Stronger than Vulcan's mighty main
Shining and bright as the light of day;
Thou dost cheer our lone pathway
With music, and a roundelay,
As sweet as bird's notes after rain!

### REPOSE.

O GLORIOUSLY perfect day!
So soft the breezes stray,
Caressingly, about our way;
And the warm sunbeams play
Around us, as in May.

The golden autumn sunshine
All nature does refine,

And her brows with glory twine;
While joy and peace divine
O'er all the scene recline.

'Tis the charm of sweet repose
The autumn round us throws,
At the busy harvest's close;
As to sleep Dame Nature goes,
Dressed in her brightest clothes.

Oh happy heart, be still!
And cease thy rapturous thrill
For joys thy cup doth fill.
Soon winter's winds will chill,
For thou art mortal, still!

I tremble for the gladness
That fills the heart to madness—
Joy more awful is than sadness!
For, even in its fullness,
It saddens by its fleetness.

## TO ADESAH N——.

I SHALL never forget our woodland rambles,
When, tired a-tramping through the brambles,
We sat down to rest on some huge, old log;
And you'd tell me stories of ships lost in fog,
Or plundered by pirates, with flag black and red,
Who, nightly, a man down their gangway led

And plunged into the deep; or gales
That veered the ships, with tattered sails,
Far from their course.   These weird tales
Held me, in strong infatuation,
Spellbound by their strange fascination.
A love for the marvelous ever was thine,
With a memory and imagination fine,
And an easy, superior style of narration.


## HOME.

IF one the comforts of a home would know,
Let him, for ten miles, face a northeast blow,
Across a prairie lone, and wild, and bleak;
No place in sight where he might even seek
Shelter and fire; the night approaching fast;
The dull November sky with clouds o'ercast;
The road so dim that he could scarcely see —
Taking the wrong one through sheer anxiety;
Tired, nervous and cold, and weary of heart,
He feels, if at home, he would never again depart.

Then, ere he knows it, let the light of home —
Brighter to him than all lights ever shone —
Shine out its welcome o'er his darkened path;
Bespeaking shelter from the night wind's wrath,
And love of her who placed it there to guide
The wand'rer safely back to his fireside:

Then if a heart e'er gratitude does know,
Or e'er with thanks to God does overflow,
His own does now, as quickly he drives in,
And sees the warmth and glow that is within.


A cheerful fire, and supper smoking hot,
Love-light in eyes still dimmed with tears, lest
    not
In safety, through the dark and stormy night,
Her loved one would return — this cheerful sight,
Heaven itself, by contrast, seems to him
Who out in the drear November night has been.
He thanks his God for the comforts of a home,
And begs His mercy upon those who roam
The weary world, in darkness and alone —
Upon whose path the light of home ne'er shone.


And so the light of heaven will, I ween,
Fall on our troubled vision, as between
This world and yon, our spirits hovering
Await the signal that our home we're nearing.
And, as the gloom and darkness were dispelled
By the light, and warmth, and peace of home,
    which swelled
His heart with gratitude — so even then,
World-worn and weary, tempest tossed again,
We'll hail with joy the beacon light of heaven,
And ne'er again by earth storms will be driven.

## DUTY.

TO A. E. N——.

"Do thy duty; that is best;
Leave unto thy Lord the rest."
— *Longfellow.*

STEADILY, steadily toiling,
Frying, and baking, and boiling—
Endless the strife and turmoiling
 Of woman's life!
Sewing, and making, and mending,
Her children's wants attending,
A round of work, unending—
 Perpetual strife!

Washing, ironing, and sweeping;
Her house in order keeping,
By slowly, surely eking
 Her strength away.
Sorely the time she's needing,
To do some little reading,
For which her mind's been pleading
 Many a day.

But all else must be attended,
The clothes all made or mended,
Or the garden neatly tended—
 She has no rest.
And *ever* something's needing;
Time flies so fast—unheeding
The heart's sad, restless pleading
 For *its* bequest.

And so a lifetime's passed!
Still, duty is the mast
Which holds her, to the last,
 Amid all trial.
Surely for her, at the gates,
The "blessed vision" waits!
For she is strong in traits
 Of self-denial.

Her hand has never stayed,
Nor duty been delayed;
Self-sacrifice she's made
 For all about her.
The needy at her door
Find bread—and evermore
She is ready to adore
 Her blessed Savior.

Sweet must be the rest,
When, at her Lord's behest,
To mansions of the blest
 Her spirit soars!
Around a life thus spent,
So earnest and intent,
A hallowed charm is lent—
 Its love outpours.

## A SKETCH.

THE light of love and gladness
   Is in her heart to-day;
The earth is filled with beauty
   And a merry roundelay.

The air is soft and perfumed,
   As from orchards blooming nigh;
While overhead, so calmly,
   The fleecy clouds float high.

All life is set to music —
   A poem sweet and rare;
For the love that is in her heart
   Makes all the earth so fair.

Her golden curls are loosened —
   The rose blooms in her cheeks;
And sitting, softly singing,
   Her glance the gateway seeks.

In joyful expectation,
   For the ideal of her heart —
At the coming of whose footsteps,
   Her happy pulses start.

But who is that she sees,
   With step slow and unsteady?
Why are her cheeks so blanched —
   Her welcome so unready?

Surely it is not he
  Of whom she has been dreaming!
This reeling, muttering man —
  And yet it has his seeming.

  *     *     *     *     *     *

Hast thou ever known a sorrow
That like a sharp-toothed harrow
  Strikes into the very soul?
Whose blighting frosts, so sere,
Wither each promise dear,
  And shatter ev'ry idol?

With outstretched arms didst cry,
"Is there a God? then why
  Such bitter suffering?"
Then only canst thou know
The depths of human woe,
  By thine own measuring.

  *     *     *     *     *     *

"Surely it is a dream,
  This awful, crushing sorrow—
Things are not what they seem —
  'Twill all be right to-morrow!

"And I, in love's delirium,
  So happy I could soar
To skies empyrean,
  A few short weeks before —

"Now to suffer like this!
　　Suddenly to have fallen
Into the dark abyss
　　Of almost hopeless woe!
'Tis like to being driven
　　Into Phlegethon low,
After a glimpse of heaven."

\*　　\*　　\*　　\*　　\*　　\*

The years have come and gone:
　　And a tired woman sits
Wearily watching the door,
　　As silently she knits.

Gone is the bloom from her cheeks —
　　A haggard look they wear;
No more the earth is blooming,
　　In fragrance, everywhere.

The song, so blithe and free,
　　Long ago died out of her heart;
At every sound she hears,
　　She gives a nervous start —

For with fear, instead of longing,
　　His coming, now, she waits;
Harsh words, instead of loving,
　　She now anticipates.

The sky is blue above her —
　　The fleecy clouds roll high;

But no longer orchard blossoms
　　Waft their sweet fragrance nigh.

For the beautiful home is gone—
　　A sacrifice to drink;
And of sky and air about her,
　　She does not care to think.

For all the light and gladness
　　Have fled from out her life;
And only pain and sadness
　　Remain—and weary strife.

Still true to the pledge she gave him,
　　When by his side a bride—
"For weal or woe I take thee,
　　Whatever may betide."


## CHANGE.

AFTER many years we meet again,
Upon life's mighty, restless main—
Amid other scenes and stranger ones—
After the cycle of many suns.

Each notes a change he cannot tell
In words, though analyzing well
The other's every tone and look,
As if reviewing a much-loved book.

O time! O change! how ruthlessly
Thou tearest the bonds of sympathy,
Of hearts that did so joyously
Fulfill each other's moiety.

Is it that one has graver grown
Because his youthful hopes have flown?
Or has the other one grown sordid,
Because of treasure he has hoarded?

Ah! both have changed, as all must change
Who on time's seething tidal range;
Youth's impulse warm, and hopefulness,
Give place to care or selfishness:

Except in natures rare and sweet,
Whose hearts with love are so replete,
That all life's storms and icy blasts,
Their gentle love cannot out cast.

## LINES TO MY MOTHER,

### WITH A WREATH OF RIPENED GRAIN, UPON HER BIRTHDAY, OCTOBER 29, 1885.

THIS ripened grain fit emblem is to thee,
Of a life well spent and full of charity.
  The wreath that encircles thy plate:
    Thy endless love, innate,
    For children, friends and mate.

These immortelles: the influence thou hast
        wrought
Upon our lives, which thou hast ever sought
    To gently guide aright.
    Surely thy crown is bright —
    To thee shall be no night!


May the golden Indian summer of thy life
Be free from toil and care and worldly strife;
    Full of the sweet repose
    That a godly life bestows,
    E'en to life's very close!


Accept this from thy absent, loving one,
Who'd crown thee with the brightness of the sun
    If it were hers to give —
    And years, for thee to live,
    Outnumbering the sands that sieve
    The passing hours of time.
    I reach my hand to thine
    And greet thee, mother mine!
    Though weary miles between
    Us now do intervene.
    Across all time and space
    I see thy smiling face;
    Our hands now interlace —
    Our loving hearts embrace!
    By loving ties so blest,
    I am,
              Your own CELESTE.

## NO NEW THING UNDER THE SUN.
ECCLESIASTES, FIRST CHAPTER.

THERE's "no new thing under the sun!"
Men are born, grow up and marry—
For a little while they tarry,
And then their race is run.
And all one can say or do
Long ago has been gone through—
For there's nothing new under the sun.

Why strive we so earnestly,
Wrestle so arduously?
For life, at its best,
Is a little boon—
Gone so soon!

The rivers run to the sea,
Yet fill it not;
The crooked cannot straightened be—
Sad is our lot!
Wisdom, itself, is vanity,
And fame an unreality,
And all a sad fatality!

No matter if there's nothing new under the sun—
Great things men are learning, one by one!
And life is a blessing,
Twice worth possessing;
Then cheerfully run

14

Till the race is done,
Filling your mission —
Then reap the fruition,
Of God's "Well done."

As the rivers flow into the sea,
Although they fill not,
They gladden most bounteously
The land throughout.
What though the crooked and straight
Together must grow!
What though our hearts must wait,
Oft burdened, below!
The bitter and the sweet
In every life must meet,
Till eternity we know.

Then laugh at pain,
And wisdom gain,
That far exceedeth folly;
Just after rain
'Tis bright again —
Indulge not melancholy.


## WAITING.

The lamps are all shining and bright,
The house all set aright,
For he's coming home to-night —

The absent one so dear,
For whom the fire burns clear —
And the hearth is clean and bright.

The snowy cloth is laid,
The table all arrayed
With the best things, on parade;
  While viands choice and rare,
  The loving hands prepare
For him who's still delayed.

The doorway oft is sought,
With loving eyes and thought,
To scan the road, lest not
  His coming be discerned —
  And oft away are turned,
Disappointed, seeing naught.

The flush of expectancy,
The eyes' deep brilliancy,
Tell the restless anxiety,
  As the hours glide on apace,
  And her heart keeps time and pace,
As the day wanes rapidly.

At last, through the even-tide
Twilight, there is descried
A carriage large and wide,
  Which "surely is the 'mail'
  A-coming from the 'rail,'
With the loved for our fireside."

All now is bustle and glee,
To see who first will be
To greet the absentee;
   But the carriage goes swiftly along,
   Leaving them standing alone,
Dejected, despondently.

The bright eyes fill with tears,
And hearts with gloomy fears —
Foreboding ill appears.
   "He will not come to-night —
   And what if our longing sight
Ne'er again meet his that cheers."

The brightness that's within
Seems mockery, akin
To sacrilegious sin;
   For may be, even now,
   The proud head's lying low,
'Mid accident's sad din.

But hark! the dog is barking,
Such sad thoughts interlarding —
The whir of wheels fast coming.
   Quickly the fire's replenished;
   And gloomy forebodings banished;
With hope the heart's high beating.

Soon a well-known voice is heard,
And the joy, so long deferred,
Is here: like a weary bird,

She nestles in loving arms,
Free from sad fear's alarms—
And thanks God her prayer was heard.

## TO MADGE.

ACROSS the table at which I sit writing,
A dear brown head is bent,
So busily intent
Upon something she, too, is carefully writing.

Her cheeks are flushed, her dark eyes bright
With thoughts that seem to please her;
And smiles the sweet lips stir.
What is my little girl writing to-night?

"I am writing poems, too!
And one, dear mamma, just for you;
But not as yours, so good all through!"

Ah! thanks my child, for your loving lays!
And thank you, too, for fulsome praise!
I'll prize them both, through all my days.
God guide your feet in wisdom's ways—
Is what a loving mother prays;
And wishes, too, her little essays
Critics as kind might find always.

## DAY-DAWN.

"THE night is far spent—
　The day is at hand;"
Already is lent
　A charm to the land,
From the roseate glow
　In the eastern sky,
By which we may know
　That the day is nigh.

The day, with its glory,
　Its freedom and light,
Will tell a new story,
　And banish the night
Of dark superstition
　And ignorance's blight,
And bring to fruition
　Our plans for the right.

And woman, no longer,
　A chattel shall be
To him who is stronger,
　But she shall be free:
By her own volition,
　To her talent and taste
She shall choose a vocation—
　Nor time shall she waste.

Because that, forsooth,
　A woman alone

Can attend the fine woof
  And the fixtures of home,
Is no reason why—
  Whether suited or not—
All should housekeeping try,
  And choose the same lot,—

Any more than at farming
  All our brothers should toil;
While truly alarming
  Would be the turmoil,
If they all the same work
  Were obliged to seek—
Else be called a shirk—
  An existence to eke.

Let her lecture and preach
  In her voice soft and sweet:
Let her "doctor" and teach,
  With dexterity neat:
She will be just as kind
  When you're sick or in need—
Truest help you will find;
  Then bid her—"God speed."

And, when the full noon-day
  In glory shall shine,
'Twill show woman the true way
  Her love to entwine
Round the inmates of home,
  Whose queen she shall be—
Her mind its great dome
  And sweet sanctity.

## TO NELLIE R. B——.

Most precious to me,
Is the sweet memory
Of the evenings when we
Discussed, socially,
Dickens's great powers,
And the mellow bellflowers!
Fast flew the hours;
For employment like ours
  Lends wings to time.

The flavor of the fruit
In richness just did suit
The books we so enjoyed —
And neither ever cloyed.
And thy fair, Saxon face,
Alive with thought and grace —
Its violet eyes
Like deep-tinted skies —
Gave coloring rich,
As, in musical pitch,
You read "Dombey and Son,"
Or the "Pickwick" fun.
Companionship like thine
I would were ever mine.
Accept this little rhyme
For the sake of "Auld Lang Syne."

## CHRISTMAS.

"CHRISTMAS is really coming,"
  Even out here in the West!
And bright eyes already are summing
  Up things they would like to have best.

And loving hands busy preparing
  Gifts for chidren and friends;
For 'tis this giving and sharing
  The charm to Christmas day lends.

Of all glad days 'tis the gladdest,
  And fullest of joy and delight:
God pity the poor, who are saddest,
  And help us make their hearts light.

Years ago, when the sweet superstition,
  Of a veritable Santa Claus, kind,
With the wand of a mighty magician —
  Who rode on the waves of the wind,

Scattering gifts everywhere as he went,
  With his sleigh and reindeers fleet,
On his gladdening errands intent—
  Held our thoughts in thrall so sweet.

How well I remember the hurry
  We children were in to peep;
We could scarcely wait, in our flurry,
  For a fire in the fire-place deep;

15

For downstairs by the chimney-side,
  Our stockings were hung at night,
That down the flue so wide,
  He could easily alight.

Even yet I have not outgrown
  The glad curiosity,
Which at Christmas dawn is known,
  To see what Santa Claus brought me.

A merry Christmas greeting
  To my many friends so true!
Wishing many a gladsome meeting,
  And many things bright and new.


## A WINTER SONG.

THE winter is here,
  With all its good cheer,
And long, pleasant evenings' delight.
  The chores are all done,
  And one by one,
Each joins the home circle bright.

  Without it may blow,
  And toss the snow;
Within all is warmth and light.
  And joy and mirth,
  Around the hearth,
Make happy hearts to-night,

As, with joyous song,
Time speeds along,
Filled with pleasant recreation.
Long tales are read,
And lessons had
For the morrow's recitation.

And corn is popped,
And nuts are cracked;
And riddles, in prose and rhyme,
Are guessed and guessed,
Until, at last,
They are told it is bed-time.

The hours pass
Too fast, alas!
'Tis bed-time ere they're ready.
O, happy time!
A golden rhyme
Are winter's pleasures, surely.

## A PRAYER.

O Thou great, loving Heart,
Throbbing with tenderness,
Look down upon us now,
Forgive our waywardness!

The hidden fires within
Our natures frighten us;

Like craters, bursting forth
From slumbering volcanoes.

With saddened hearts we throw
Ourselves upon Thy grace;
With choking sobs we bow —
O let us see thy face!

Thy works are glorious —
This world so beautiful;
All things declare Thy praise,
Only man is sinful!

He, who should praise the most —
So slow Thy will to know!
O help us keep the paths
We know we ought to go!

## THE NEW YEAR.

THE New Year with its hopes and fears,
Its promises of joy and tears —
A welcome, yet a dreaded host —
Is waiting like a silent ghost.

O, if we did its secrets know,
Whether it held more joy or woe
For us poor tenants here below,
Warmer greeting we might bestow:

Or else, in terror, might recoil
From all the sorrow and turmoil
We'd see for us was held in store,
And shrink, faint-hearted, e'en before

It was begun: so that, in this,
A state of "Ignorance is bliss."
But fair thy promises, O Year!
We'll trust thee, then, nor think of fear.

Good-by, Old Year! that just is done —
Too quickly and full well you've run
Your mission here. We had our share
Of pleasure — and we grateful are.

With high resolves, and courage true,
And hopefulness, we'll greet the New;
And pray that, sparingly, He'll deal
Our sorrows — bountifully, our weal.


GROWING OLD.

How fast time flies! And we're growing old!
The summer's past, and the winter's cold
Withers the flowers along our path,
And we gather, instead, the aftermath.

Not so fragrant and fresh as the first glad crop
Of youthful hopes, in which there's no drop

Of doubt or fear but the world will prove
All one desires, as onward we move;

But mixed with the seeds of honest doubt
Whether our plans will be carried out;
And whether there's more of pleasure or pain,
Even when our best hopes we proudly attain.

The joyous enthusiasm of youth
Is gone—but replaced by the riper truth
Of sober and well-earned experience;
And we look on life's failures with lenience.

The youthful glamour no longer deceives;
Life's earnest endeavor no longer leaves
Us time in a fanciful world to live:
For to our life's work each thought we must
    give.

When our heads like the "almond tree shall
    flourish,"
And plans for this world no longer we cherish—
May our lives be like a well-linked chain,
As memory goes back to trace them again.

And when, at the last, the "silver cord
Is loosed," and we go to our reward—
May some noble deed we did while here
To our jeweled crown add one brilliant more.

## IN MEMORIAM.

DEAR baby Ethlyn,
　My wee, sweet flower!
Thy memory, even,
　Is a priceless dower.
Ere thou wert born
　I loved thee well;
Like the light of morn
　Thy coming fell
Across our way,
　A rosy light,
For a brief stay —
　Then all was night.

And bitter at first
　Our heart-aches were;
A hunger and thirst
　Our souls did stir,
For a love as sweet
　As the roses' breath:
It did not seem meet
　That thou, O death,
Shouldst claim so soon
　Our birdling dear —
The lovely bloom
　Which would so cheer

Our lonely hearts.
　But now, at last,
Though the teardrop starts,
　The bitter is past:

For, in gardens fairer,
  Our flowret is blooming,
And a love, much rarer
  Than of our bestowing,
Is given to her
  In that realm of light—
And we cannot demur
  At her spirit's flight.


## CONTRAST.

Even as I hear the wild winds blow,
Tossing the restless, shifting snow,
Hurling it hard 'gainst the window pane,
Dashing it here and thither again,
Moaning and howling where'er they go:
In contrast sweet, there comes a scene
Of verdant meads and forests green,
Fragrant flowers and song of birds,
Flowing waters and lowing herds—
All the beauty of summer's sheen.
I see again the deep blue skies,
Fair as a maiden's azure eyes;
And hear the drowsy hum of bees,
Or gentle swaying of the trees,
As through their leaves the south wind sighs.

O can this be the same glad world,
Now the storm king fierce has hurled

All his furious, biting blast
'Gainst our beauteous scene? and vast
Storms and tempests he has unfurled?

And so, when the storms of life beat hard
Upon the thoughtful, sensitive bard,
He wonders at the glorious dreams
That came to him with morning's beams—
Waving, beckoning him fancy-ward;
And muses long on the mystery
Of life's ever-changing history—
The subtle workings of love and joy,
And bitter cares which so annoy,
Later on, upon life's rough sea.
He knows that in some way the earth's renewed
By the frost, and snow, and tempests rude;
And that summer skies will come once more
With beauty and gladness as before—
And all our way with flowers be strewed.

Then, when our mental sky is o'ercast
By troubles dark, and angry blast,
Let us endure; and cherish the thought
That out of it all some good will be wrought—
And wintry storms will not always last.

## TWIN LAKES.
### VISITED AUGUST 10, 1877.

Twin sisters—recluses!
Fit founts for the Muses,
Or fair water-sprite,

Are thy cool waters bright.
Around thy sacred quiet
Spirits of beauty riot.
White mountain peaks, and cóld,
In stately grandeur, hold
Their constant silent watches —
Guarding thy lovely couches.

They are vigilant warders
Around thy green borders —
Whose cares never slack;
And you pay them back
By reflecting their fairness
Within your own clearness;
E'en their purple and gold
Your limpid waters mold
Into beauty fairer,
And a grandeur rarer:

As thy sun-kissed surface
Mirrors back the surplus
Of beauty the sky bestowed,
And fleecy, sun-lined cloud;
And the sun's own brilliance,
From thy deep waters, hence,
Scatters in golden beams,
Till the scene like heaven seems,
As slowly in our boat,
We glide o'er these waters remote.
Around, above, below,
Visions of beauty glow,
As in one's brightest dream —
And silence reigns supreme.

## THE CITIES' POOR.

WRITTEN AFTER READING A SPEECH BY HON. T. B. STUART,
OF DENVER, COL., ENTITLED "THE WORKER'S SITUATION."

### I.

'Tis dawn! The heart of the great city beats
With quick'ning pulse, that has a few hours stayed
Its restless throbbings. In gray and misty dawn
The light contends with darkness, work with rest.
In musty cellar, and in dingy loft,
The weary toilers of the city wake
To renew again the hard, unequal fight
Of labor 'gainst the grim wolf at the door.
Pallid and careworn, in the dim March light,
They eat their scanty meal, and then betake
Themselves, unrested, to their daily toil —
Thin-clad and pinched for want of fire and food.
A father and his son — a lad of twelve,
Sad-eyed, and grown much older than his years —
Go down into the jetty mines of coal,
Where, early and late, denied the blessed sun,
They labor hard for a mere paltry sum,
On which to eke a poor existence out.
A widow with a little, helpless brood,
Trudges along through damp and smoky air,
To leave the children at a "nursery farm,"
While she by factory work their living earns;
Treading the weary way again at night,
To take them to her dismal upper room.
Another less self-sacrificing one
Turns them with a crust into the street;

For safer there she deems her little ones,
Than locked in their own old, rickety room.
The street's poor nursery for these little waifs —
No wonder that they learn deceit and sin.
And all day long these mothers toil for bread
With weary hands, and heads and hearts that ache.
Young women, and little girls of even eight,
Sit all day long at toil unfit for youth —
Like flowers blighted ere 'tis time to bloom —
Grown old and haggard at the spool and loom,
For just enough to poorly live upon.

## II.

Can you wonder at the muttered discontent,
The lowering cloud grown darker with the years —
The ills of these poor people giving vent
In mobs and strikes, in curses and in tears?
The crowded city's poor, so poorly fed —
Can they be freemen, while they're slaves for bread?
Would they, like valiant soldiers, fight for homes,
When they have none but dim and dusty rooms? —
Be leal and loyal to their country's flag,
When they for clothes have but a flimsy rag?
Can we a nation build that's strong and great,
When the foundation stones are in this state?
The top must totter when the base decays;
And he who would build strongly first lays
The true and firm foundation — then he builds
With ease and certainty against all ills.
While rich our land in acres broad and deep,
Shall these lack homes, and in confusion steep

Our country, boasted free?  Shall English earls,
Or corporate bodies, or old, wealthy churls,
In large estates, our glorious country hold,
While millions of our poor, in want untold,
Have not a foot of ground to call their own?
Then, truly, the glory of our land is flown.
Awake, fair land! Columbia wake, and claim
Your lawful right of "eminent domain!"
Give each a home on these broad prairies green,
And this the picture that will then be seen:
Let stout and well-paid hands both spin and
    weave,
But give the million weaklings sweet reprieve;
And let the factory's poor and pallid ones
Seek the green fields, and cheering, bright'ning
    suns.
The season may be spring — the morning damp;
They rise at dawn, but not to chill and cramp;
You hear them singing; for their cheerful toil
Speaks more of lusty life than hard turmoil.
The father yokes his oxen; while the son —
The once pale lad, grown stout, and brown with
    tan —
Attends the cow, and carries the brimming pail
Into the humble home; where the once frail
And weary mother, freshened by pure air,
Bestirs herself with breakfast's dainty fare —
The rich, sweet milk, and eggs just newly lain,
And bread as smooth and white as porcelain.
The meal dispatched, they hasten to their work —
But not through sloppy street, or city's smoke —

Past green wheat fields, where birds are singing
    loud,
To black, rich soil all ready to be plowed;
The sun's bright rays dispelling fast the dew,—
All form a scene to them so bright and new,
They wonder if Aladdin's lamp they've found,
And now are living on enchanted ground.
Across the way, the widow and her girls,
With cheeks now blooming, and with tossy curls,
Attend the poultry and their small-fruit patch;
Or train the morning-glories o'er the thatch.
Instead of the mill's incessant click-clack,
The happy hens sing, " Cut-cut, cut-cut, cut-tack; "
And the guineas chime in, " Pot-rack, buckwheat,
    pot-rack."
They breathe, instead of greasy, smoky air,
Odor of fresh-turned earth and flowers fair;
And hail with joy the copious spring showers,
That fill the earth with gladness and with flowers.
Is not this scene of pleasant, thrifty toil,
Happier far than the great city's moil?
And they who in the factories have stayed
Are better off, because they're better paid;
While thousands, who once toiled to gain their
    bread,
And went half clad and homeless, poorly fed,
Have plenty now, and some to spare instead.
With homes that are their own, and grown so dear,
The Nation, for her safety, need not fear;
For if she ever needs strong, loyal hands,
She'll find them in these sons who till the lands.

## BALANCE ROCK, COLORADO.

THOU giant rock,
So neatly balanced between earth and sky!
What fateful shock
Left thee a wonder to the passers by?

How many centuries hast thou withstood
The ravages of time, and wind, and flood?
And what will be the power to make thee yield—
To lay thou proud head low upon the field?
Or art so evenly balanced, after all,
That man nor time shall ever see thee fall?

O mortal, balanced between right and wrong,
Resist all influence, however strong,
To topple thee from manhood's towering height
Into the dust and debris, far from sight!
And pray for power to discriminate
The circumstance which weakens thy estate—
Whether it be a power small or great—
And changes, e'en for life and death, thy fate.


## SONGS THAT WILL LIVE.

No GLITTERING array of idle words,
Though musical as the song of birds,
    Can e'er attract the busy herds
Of men who labor hard to gain
The summit of this earthly fane,
    And have no time for many words.

But thoughts that glow with warmth and fire,
Inspiring men to climb still higher,
 And on the rugged path ne'er tire; —
These are the words that true help give,
And these the songs that long will live,
 After all lighter ones expire.

If thou hast a yearning, then,
To live in the hearts of thy fellow-men,
 Make real and useful what you pen;
Fill every picture with the fire and glow
Of thoughts and emotions that overflow
 Your own soul's inmost ken.

The sympathy and help which most are prized
Come from those who have realized
 The same great joy, or the agonized
Sense of suffering and bitter loss,
Which separates the gold from dross —
 Comfort like this is well assized.

Then, with truth and all sincerity,
In meekness and simplicity,
 And yet not with timidity,
Sing the songs of joy and gladness,
And the soft refrains of sadness —
 Give to each heart sympathy.

# LOVE PURIFIED.

My object in writing this not altogether fanciful sketch, has been to warn my own sex from the sin to which she is most easily prone—idolatry of loved ones and beautiful surroundings. And, while I have instanced one blessed with the greatest luxuries of life, it may be very nearly as applicable to those in the humbler walks of life, as it is a passion which the circumstances and ideas of the present day seem to cultivate and intensify in all. Hence I dedicate this—

> To Woman—purest, fairest of creation—
> The blessing or the blight of ev'ry station!
> Beloved of God, and angels, and of men;
> O see that thou love purely, wisely, then!

CELESTE MAY.

## LOVE PURIFIED.

T'was on a spot as fair as e'er the sun
In all his warmth and splendor shone upon
The young bride found her pleasant future home,
Prepared by loving hands, ere she should come.
Its marble walls stood glist'ning through the
    green
Of tropic trees, while fountain sprays were seen
Scattering their sparkling diamonds o'er a lawn
Which rivaled, in its brightness, glorious dawn.

17

A range of mountains, in the distance, lay
In gold and purple shadows' bright array;
The lucid waters of a lake, serene,
Were gleaming, in the sunshine white, between;
And air as fragrant as the flowers' breath
Pervaded all the place: above, beneath,
Wherever one might look—the spirit fair,
Of love and beauty, had its dwelling there.

To Laura, loved and loving, it all seemed
To far surpass all she had ever dreamed—
E'en in her girlish and most lavish dreams—
Of elegance combined with beauteous scenes.
And it was hers—the gift of priceless love!—
O dared a spirit not yet gone above
Revel in beauty and a perfect love?—
For she, though gently reared, had yet been
    taught,
With Puritanic strictness, that the thought
Must soar above all earthly loves, lest aught
Of worship for them bring one's hopes to naught;
And, that 'twas virtue, when the soul acquired
Strength to refuse the things it most desired,
No matter what they were—e'en half inspired.
Heroic, but a rigid, austere creed,
Sav'ring too much of the self-penance deed
Of old, ascetic monks, of whom we read.

And Laura, all her life, had been at war
With this, which seemed her great besetting sin:
The love of beauty, seen in earth or star,

The glory of the sunset cloud, or in
The bright, sweet flowers, which many a rough
    place
Soften and smooth by their bewitching grace,
A perfect face or beautiful attire—
All seemed to satisfy that inward fire
Which burned within her heart, without desire
Or envious longing to possess them all;
O could she, by so pure a love, e'en fall?
In vain herself she chided—it was born
Within her; she could not uproot this thorn.
A simple child of nature—one withal
Too rarely found! and now, by love's sweet thrall,
She finds the grandeur of the earth her own;
And what is dearer far to her than all,
The noble love of one fit for a throne.

No wonder, then, that at the first a dread
Lest all this beauty turn her heart and head
Should cast a shadow o'er her happy brow:
For "Coming events, before, their shadows
    throw."
'Twas not the nature of a mind like this
To long withstand the influence of such bliss—
Where e'en the fragrant air seemed heaven's kiss.
Her innate love of beauty so intense,
Her early training was but poor defense;
And, half in fear, and half in defiance,
She thought: "Why did God such beauty then
    bestow,
If 'tis so great a sin to love it so?

And why this world He with such beauty clothes,
If not to be admired and loved by those
Who dwell upon it?"—and thus deeper stole
Into her heart the idol of her soul.
Ah! happier had it been for her, by far,
If still she worshiped beauty from afar,
With no indulgence or excess to mar
So fine an ideal of true beauty's star.
But lulled by bliss, and love, and sweet repose,
Slowly, but surely, she more careless grows
Of the true worship, which should ever flow
To the Creator of our gifts, and glow
High above every other love we know.
Her energy and being concentrate
On making her already blest estate
Happier still, and still more enchanting,
By adding every charm of artist's skill,
To touch the sense of beauty by their thrill;
Or her own potent charm still more enhancing,
To make the love she knows already hers
Hers indissolubly, by all that stirs
The heart to admiration, and endears.

And thus the sweet idolatry enthralls
Ere she's aware, who by its spell thus falls
Into forgetfulness of former things,
As deep and sure as draughts from Lethe
        brings; —
Yet her enchantment should be likened more
To eating the sweet fruit the Lotus bore,
Instead of dark draughts from the infernal shore.

Months, years, elapse; and, though the fear
That all this wealth of pleasure, grown so dear,
Would sometime have an end, came far too near
For peace of mind or comfort, 'twas banished ere
One earnest thought had left its impress there.
Until at last, by sickness smitten down,
The lovely, placid brow by pain is drawn,
And all sweet sounds and beauty cannot drown
The saddened thoughts that on her mind now
    dawn;
But not through selfishness this sadness came—
Too pure for that, e'en yet, her spirit's flame—
But O, a heart and home left desolate,
Where love had reigned supreme—too cruel
    fate!
A yearning, tender pity filled her heart,
Like angels feel, who from the heavens dart,
On errands of mercy to poor mortals sent—
To comfort and console, their sweet intent;
'Twas thus her heart—though just upon the rim
Of ceaseless, unknown shores—turned now to
    him
Whose cup of sorrow's filled e'en to the brim,
And wishes she might stay to comfort him.

She did not worry about her own state,
Though, so indifferent, she had been of late
To all she had been taught to venerate;
For had she not, e'en in her infancy,
Been taught to love and reverence Deity,
And dream of long and blessed eternity,

Until it was, to her, a natural trait
To think of heaven's joys as her own right?
And now, the light of life was going out,
She would not let a flitting, ill-timed doubt
Her life-long hopes and expectations blight.
In all her fond, ambitious wandering,
She never to herself dared intimate
That God she was no longer worshiping,
But at a shrine she did herself create—
A beautiful, but transient, earthly fane,
Which brought her, now, no strength'ning for
    the pain
Of threat'ning dissolution, and the parting
From all her earthly loves; so, once again,
She turns her mind to Him, who, in her youth
Had been to her the Essence of all Truth;
And tries to summon back that restful faith,
To give her strength to meet death's dreaded
    wraith.

Ah! such is ever sinful man's presumption,
Based on the loving, holy Christ's redemption:
While health and beauty lavishly are given,
He turns his thoughts to all else but to heaven;
But when affliction's icy hand he feels,
And the warm blood, slowly, in his veins congeals,
He quickly turns his thoughts to the Rock riven
That all his wanderings might be forgiven;
That great and loving Heart that ever feels
A throb of sympathy for man, and seals
Our pardon, through the leniency of Heaven.

'Tis growing dark! and she no longer feels
The loving touch and pressure of the hand
Of that dear one, who by the bedside kneels.
She tries to speak, but can no longer make
A word or wish of hers articulate
To loving years of those who vainly try
Her ev'ry whispered word to understand.
She hears the sweep of angels' wings close by,
And thinks, "They've come to bear me to the
    sky."
Sweet music—faint and far, then coming near—
Seems wafted to her from the heavenly sphere,
Richer than ever mortal ears could hear.
An intense yearning fills her soul to go
Where she that perfect harmony, too, shall know,
And revel ever in its melodious flow:
Surely one need not look on death with dread—
They were the living, we on earth the dead.
An icy numbness all her senses drank—
A sigh, a shiver, and then all was blank.


Long hours have elapsed, and she again
Awakes to consciousness; but there's no pen
Or words to tell the awful, burning pain,
Or fancies of that fever-maddened brain.
Instead of heavenly vistas, brighly glowing,
Through which the limpid water of life is flow-
    ing,
And glorious strains from angel voices sweet,
And golden pavements 'neath her trembling
    feet—

Instead of glories she had hoped to see
Upon the vast shores of eternity,
Of which she just had caught a glimmering,
As of a light on crystal waters shimmering—
Accustomed things appear unto her eyes,
Although to shut them out, in vain, she tries.
For, vividly, she remembers she had died—
Had bade, to each, a last and fond farewell—
Had heard the rushing wings of Azrael;
And had he, all these hours, so vainly tried
To waft her soul away from earthly-tide?
The needed mystic word had not been given,
Which plumes the soul for its swift flight to
         heaven.


And now, the burning pain in limbs and brain
Tells, all too plainly, that the soul again
Is close allied to suff'ring, moldering clay;
And that, of all heaven's brightness, not a ray
Could ever o'er her sinful being stray.
It seemed the home, on which she once had spent
Her ev'ry thought and energy intent—
Her all of love and worship—was to be,
In spite of longing prayers to heaven sent,
Her only home through all eternity.


Her fate was horrible; oblivion sweet
Compared to punishment like this, so meet:
Forever dying, yet not to die, her doom;
Chained, soul and body, to this favorite room;

Hideous and loathsome, ever lying there,
A stagnant blot upon the once pure air
Of home—a clog to him she'd held so dear.
The bitterness of her lot was made more keen
By the glimpses of fair heaven she had seen.

A creature neither fit for earth nor heaven —
To whom no burial, even, could be given!
The home and friends that she had loved *too*
    much,
She feared would be polluted by her touch,
And tried, in vain, to hide away from sight,
Longing for power to flee in the dark night,
And in the cool, clear waters, far away,
Her anguished, fevered body grateful lay;
Content to lie there and forgotten be
Through all the cycles of eternity,
If, in this way, her loved ones she might free.

O that the earth beneath her would be riven,
And hide her from the sight of home and Heaven —
To which she dared not pray to be forgiven!
For when life's current warm her pulse had
    thrilled,
And joy and pleasure's cup had e'en been filled
To overflowing, how careless she had grown
In sending petitions to a heavenly throne;
And now to pray seemed mockery, akin
To vilest and most sacrilegious sin.
The voluptuous pleasures of her home, too well
She loved—and thus, in blindly loving, fell.

18

The idol of her heart had been her home;
Now, dead and living both, it was her tomb.


And thus, for weary weeks she lay and tossed,
Thinking herself a spirit doomed and lost.
Remorse stirred deep within her troubled breast —
So weary, yet she never hoped for rest:
For, ever and again her mind went back
To "Heaven lost because of faith so slack."
The good things God had loaned her to be used,
She had, through blind idolatry, abused.
How plainly, now, she saw the narrow way,
From which, by flowers, she'd been led astray.
O if she could but bathe her burning brow
In the cool waters that through Eden flow,
Or look one moment on the living tree
That gives to all blest immortality,
Gladly she'd give up now all past delight,
For just one glimpse of this fair, heavenly sight,
That to her longing heart seems to enhance,
Now she shall never view its vast expanse.


In her sad state of mental aberration
One attribute of God she had forgotten —
His wondrous love — until the sweet narration
Of the forgiving words the Christ had spoken
Unto the dying thief, who at His side,
Repentant, turned to Him, the Crucified —
Dawned on her mind, as she lay deeply thinking
Upon God's awful justice, so unshrinking;
And quickly o'er the twilight darkness came

A faint but steady light of reason's flame,
Enabling her to think with more precision
Upon God's revelation unto man;
And there came thronging to her mental vision
The instances which through the Bible ran
Of wondrous, mighty things that Faith had
    wrought —
That loving, entire faith which ever brought
Fulfillment of the blessing it had sought.
What God had done, would He not do again?
Could He not speak the word, and give her, then,
New life — e'en had she died a hundred times?
And Faith reëchoed, "Yea, a hundred times!"
And with the rest this trustful feeling brings
Come natural thoughts of man and earthly things.
Faith, talismanic word — the Christian's sun —
Dispelled the dark'ning shadows that had run
Through all her fancies; again bright reason
    shone
Where long it had been tottering on its throne,
Enshrouded by a self-accusing gloom;
And reawakened memory clearly came,
Lighting her mind with its resplendent flame —
She knew it all had been a feverish dream,
Through which awakened conscience shed its
    gleam;
And that it never, yet, had been God's plan,
In *such* a way, to punish sinful man.

And yet she shuddered, when she thought again
Of all those dreadful phantoms of the brain;

And how much she had needed the lesson taught,
Though by such bitter, direful chast'ning wrought.
Henceforth her faith more steadfastly should shine
Through all she did; and love and faith divine,
Produce good works—rich fruit from the true
    vine.
A prayer of thanksgiving from her heart arose,
Like none but the truly chastened spirit knows.
Hope, that eternal anchor of souls, shines through
Her soul, as she consecrates her life anew
To God, the Just One, and the Loving, too.

Impatiently she waits the coming, now,
Of loved ones lately met with moody brow;
And at whose footsteps, now, her pulses bound
With happiness, and love and life new-found.
One brief but loving glance tells all the tale—
That she no longer dwells within the vale;
Not only reason's light, within her face,
But radiant joy reflected, they can trace,
As if it came direct from heavenly grace.
O, if to mortals here there e'er is given
A foretaste of the light and love of heaven,
'Tis given them, as, back from the shadowy place,
They hold their loved once more in their embrace—
More beautiful than ever, as the grace
Of chastened love shines from her pale, sweet face.

And she!—no pardon to the guilty man
Who's saved from hanging by the merest span
Of seconds, ever made him happier than

This sweet, new lease of life does her; there thrills
A loving sympathy for all the ills
And sinfulness of man, within her heart;
For she, too, of it all has had her part,
And feels related close to human woe,
In every phase that mortals ever know.
Her life, henceforth, shall be a life of love,
But not like that from which she's just been shrove.
She knows, now, that the gifts that God has given
Are ours to love, but cannot be our heaven;
And must not come between our love for Him
Before whom all must bow — e'en seraphim;
Nor give the creature what belongs alone
To the Creator, sitting on His throne.


And now, her mind at peace, the body, too,
Erelong regains its wonted healthy hue,
And she's permitted once again to breathe
The outdoor air; and stand in awe beneath
The great, clear vault of heaven, whose tender blue
Seems smiling down upon her with a new
And purer love. 'Tis now the sweet spring-tide,
And clear voiced birds are singing far and wide;
While ev'ry tree and shrub new beauty wears —
Their bloss'ming fragrance borne on balmy airs
Like incense sweet. Earth never seemed so fair
To her, as now that she sees everywhere
The hand that made it all so bright and fair.
She loves the world, and all that is within,
With love made pure, by suffering, from sin.

## TO MY FRIEND MRS. S——.

A PRICELESS treasure is given to thee —
    A jewel bright and rare;
A cherub from the heavenly sea,
    With azure eyes and fair.

'Tis right that you should highly prize it—
    'Twas given thee to love;
Be careful not to idolize it —
    This darling, cooing dove.

And I, dear friend, rejoice with thee
    In this thy new-found joy;
May the jewel long be loaned to thee —
    This darling, precious boy.

And when he grows to man's estate,
    Most useful may he be!
Fulfilling the fond hopes, elate,
    Of thy dear maternity.


## TO THE SAME,
### UPON THE DEATH OF HER CHILD.

YOUR grief, for a time, seemed my own, dear
    friend,
And I longed with your own my tears to blend,
For a love and a life too bright to end.
To end did I say?—O 'tis just begun;
In a purer sphere shall his course be run,

Unfettered by time, with its cares and fears,
Its hopes and ambitions, and bitter tears;
These, fond mother are spared thy son.

Your flower will unfold in gardens above,
Watered and nourished by the Fountain of Love,
Sheltered securely, and never to rove.
The life, that gave promise of being so fair,
Schooled in heaven — what height may it attain
    there!
Much better God's school than our best, you
    know;
Then check the wild grief, and the tears that flow,
And think of the glory to which he is heir.

Of lone, empty arms, I, too, know the grief —
A bright jewel loaned for a space so brief —
A joy snatched away that seemed almost chief
Of the joys of life; yet I've learned to see
It was all for the best for her and me.
Thy will, Gracious Lord — may thy will be done!
And bring us, at last, through Thy Glorious One,
To join all our loved ones, and dwell with Thee.

## AT LAST.

THERE will come a morning
  On which the sun will rise,
In wonted glory crowning

The hills and fields and skies;
But to its beauties, thronging,
    Fast closed will be our eyes.

Our work will lie undone,
    Unless by others wrought;
Even when high the sun,
    There'll come no care or thought;
The well-trod paths we've run
    Must be by others sought.

Unheeding all the calls
    Of duty and of love,
Held in death's icy thralls,
    We'll lie, and cannot move,
No matter what befalls
    Those we have served in love.

Happy for us, if then
    A brighter dawn shall rise,
Than known to mortal ken,
    Or viewed by mortal eyes;
And we awake again
    'Neath heaven's glorious skies.

Happy if life's garment
    Was easily thrown by,
To don the better raiment
    Given to us on high:
Leaving earth-worn tenement
    For " mansions in the sky."

## ESTRANGED.

THE breath of flowers' sweet perfume,
And strains of music, fill the room,
As the swelling notes of the wedding march
Trill through the decorated arch
Of a stately church, in a Southern town,
Filled full to witness love's sweet crown.
Approaching the altar, the two now stand,
Sealing their vows with close-clasped hand.
He, in dark and manly beauty,
Vows to cherish in bounden duty —
To love, protect, and shield from care,
And all his earthly goods to share;
While she, so clinging and so fair,
With azure eyes and golden hair,
Robed in a silken train of white —
A vision that excels the light —
Screened by a veil of fairy gauze,
Tastefully fastened with orange blows,—
Promises, too, that no light cause
Shall ever set aside love's laws;
And that she'll honor and love alway
Him at whose side she stands to-day.

Ah, loving bonds! how light they seem,
Securely held by love's bright beam —
A chain that's woven of sweet flowers
Like fairies breathe in aerial bowers.
If bright are kept the links that bind,
These bonds may always seem as kind;

19

But love's a flower must be tended,
Or all its beauty soon is ended,
Its fragrance lost, its brightness fled,
And it lies withered, sere, and dead.
May God forbid that these two hearts
Shall e'er suffer the fiery darts
Of jealousy or dark despair,
That comes when one has ceased to care,
Or tend the beauteous flower of love,
That makes this world like that above.

\*     \*     \*     \*     \*     \*     \*     \*

A month of unalloyèd bliss
Has fled as swiftly as the kiss
Which woke Endymion, as he lay
Sleeping, far up the mountain way.
A new household now finds its place,
In love and beauty's quiet grace,
Among other homes; and there are none
With happier promise than this one:
For love and beauty here combine,
In this cottage where roses and eglantine
In graceful beauty intertwine.
Charles to his business devotes his powers;
In adorning their home, her leisure hours
Sweet Eva spends, or among her flowers,
Brightening and blessing, like summer showers.
And, in the evenings, the sweet home life
Refreshes his soul from the care and strife
Of the weary days; like heaven seems
The light that from his own hearth gleams.

Their voices in sweet song unite,
Or in some rare new book delight.
O joy! of all life's joys the sweetest,
A happy home — fullest, completest!
Would that no cloud should ever rise
To darken the brightness of their skies;
And never the first harsh look or tone
Change love's summer to colder zone:
For love, best boon to mortals given,
Is both the "way and guide" to heaven.
O cherish it from noxious blast,
For to life's ship 'tis sail and mast.

\*      \*      \*      \*      \*      \*      \*      \*

As structures great, from slightest flaws,
Are weakened, so, from smallest cause,
The even tenor of one's life
May din, discordant, with sad strife,
Which might have been avoided, had
Th' impatient word been left unsaid.
Though small the breach, widening apace,
Like streams that great divergence trace;
Or, like great fires from smallest tinder,
The first harsh word may burn to cinder
Love's rarest gem — if, by rude winds
'Tis fanned, in unforgiving minds.
And often the most loving hearts,
Too sensitive, feel keenest, darts
Intended not to wound so deep;
But, once enlodged, will ever keep
Rankling within the loving breast —
Too crucial pain to bear love's test.

And so, with these two hearts, close bound
By ties, indissolubly wound,
Who have, for years, through all the tide
Of joy and woe, walked side by side,—
Now first, by some impatience torn,
Or business cares too sadly worn,
Bestow the angry look and tone
That leaves each heart bleeding and lone.
False pride bade each one not to yield
The other this, their first-fought field.
Pride, like that by which was riven,
And lost to angels, fairest heaven,
Loses to them the quiet peace
Of a loving home; and soon they cease
The kindly care and generous thought
Which love, spontaneously, brought.
Indifference first, and then neglect—
Foul weeds—spring up, and soon reflect
Their odious coarseness on the bloom
In love's fair garden; and the gloom
Of their rank shade around is thrown,
And pois'nous pollen thither blown;
Until the garden's overgrown
With bitterness and discontent,
Where, once, a hallowed charm was lent
By tenderest love. Each one, intent
Upon his wrongs and suff'ring tense,
Knows not the others wretchedness,
But deems himself unloved—and hence
They drift apart in loneliness.

And firmer grown in this belief,
Poor Eva seeks, as some relief,
To leave the home which now but seems,
The sepulcher of fondest dreams.
But O, how cruelly it tears
Her tender heart! and, unawares,
Steals o'er her mind the real worth
Of one's own loved and treasured hearth.
But home it is no longer, where
The guiding hand of love's not there.
So, as the length'ning shadows fall,
She takes a last fond look at all:


"Farewell!—my dear old home,
  Where I so long have dwelt;
  Upon whose sacred hearth
  So often I have knelt;—
  'Neath thy kindly shelter
  So long I've waked and slept;
  Under thy dear old roof
  So oft I've joyed and wept!
      Farewell! I must say farewell,
      Though each sad sound's a knell
      To every hope of pleasure;
      Farewell, my every treasure!


"Each corner a sacred nook,
  Thy pictured walls my pride;
  Where the firelight glistened and glowed
  So oft at evening-tide!

The books that ever have brought
Sweet company and rest;
The piano, where, at twilight,
I played the songs loved best!
 Now, passionately, I play
 The old and favorite lay
 Of 'Home, Sweet Home'—
 A sob each measured tone.


"O can I say farewell
To these my cherished treasures?
To the place that's been the scene
Of my success and failures?
For years, with best endeavor,
I've sought to intertwine
Love's choicest gifts and favor
Around this earthly shrine.
 But now, a long farewell!
 No more am I to dwell
 In this my much loved home—
 A wanderer, I roam!"


And so she sang, with aching heart,
Her farewell, while the teardrops start.
She did not see where she had failed,
And all this misery entailed,
Through lack of one forgiving word
When first love's placid font was stirred
By angry words, and thoughts uncurbed,
Which all its waters left disturbed.

Now, ere the coming of the dawn,
From home and husband she had gone;
To try if thus she might forget
Her wretchedness, and live, e'en yet.
O, could she only see or know
How keenly felt this cruel blow
By him, whose love she thought was dead,
'Twould have in both hearts forgiveness plead,
And to sweet reconcilement led
These hearts that, separated, bled.

\*　　\*　　\*　　\*　　\*　　\*　　\*　　\*

The days have lengthened into weeks —
But the forgetfulness she seeks
Cannot be won.　No matter where
She comes or goes, there greets her, there,
The silent ghost of days so fair,
Ere grief had filled her heart with care.
Unable to resume once more
The pleasures which brought joy before,
She wanders restlessly, unblest,
Away from where she might have rest,
If only she'd retrace her way,
This long and lonely summer's day.


A sudden yearning fills her breast
To see once more the dear home nest,
And look again upon the face
Whose ev'ry image she can trace;
Its lines, by absence, gentler made,

And lighter—less and less of shade.
The resolution formed, she wastes
No time in faltering, but hastes
At swiftest speed, on early train—
Ere courage fail or day shall wane—
Her destination, fair, to gain.
And, just as twilight shadow lends
A tender charm to all, she bends
Her eager footsteps to the spot
Where once so blessed had been her lot.
The door's ajar, the window raised;
She hears a voice, and starts, amazed
At hearing, in a low, sad strain,
Her own name breathed in soft refrain:
"O Eva! come to me again!

   "How desolate these bowers
      That once were gay!
   How withered are the flowers,
      Now she's away,
   Who lovingly bestowed
      The tender care
   By which they grew and glowed
      With color rare!
   How lonely are these walls—
      Their beauty gone!
   Startled my own footfalls—
      Treading alone,
   Where two were wont to walk
      At twilight's hour,
   And in sweet converse talk
      In this fair bower.

How dark and still the place —
   It's life all dead,
Since she who gave it grace
   Has from it fled!
A boat with but one oar,
   On midnight sea! —
I ne'er knew gloom before —
   Ah! woe is me!
I would that I had died
   Ere first I said
Those angry words of pride —
   Swift arrows sped,
Unheeding what betide."

She listens, breathless, to the end;
Did guardian angels her thus send
To hear these words that tell her still
She's loved and missed?  A happy thrill
Steals through her frame; and at a bound
She's at his side — her arms are wound
About his neck in sweet caress
And pity for his loneliness.
"Forgive!" "Forgive!" they utter, both,
The word they had so long been loth
To speak.  The noblest word on earth —
A rare, bright gem, of heavenly birth!

20

## LONGFELLOW.

As AMPHION, by the music of his lyre,
Built mighty walls about the ancient Thebes,
E'en so didst thou, in beauty, build a higher,
From which all glory of the sky and glebes,
E'en by the common mind can be discerned—
Guided by thy unerring, gifted pen.
The lowliest theme was never by thee spurned,
Yet heavenly fire within thy pictures burned.
"The Great Interpreter!" well hast thou earned
The title: for, unto thy fellow-men,
Thou didst show the beauty of familiar things
So little thought of, and less understood;
Didst bring from far and near most joyful tidings,
To ev'ry human heart, in ev'ry mood!


## BRYANT.

PROPHET and faithful priest of nature, thou,
Who didst, at woodland altars, ever bow
In love, and praise, and adoration sweet!
Thy heart in happy unison did beat
With loving nature, throbbing round thy feet
In flowing stream, or forest's cool retreat,
The sky's rich tinted hues at sunsets glow,
Or zephyrs sighing through the leaflets, low;

The mountains—all of earth, or air, or sky,
Their secrets yielded their true votary!
The glossy green of forest leaves, the blue
Of summer skies, the morn and eve's bright hue,
And ladened bee, are seen as one reads through
His book, as fresh and fragrant as the dew.


## LIGHT.

"LET there be light!" God said, "and there was
    light!"
And it dispelled the chaos of the night
Which long had brooded, darkling, o'er the earth,
From its conception till its glorious birth.
His own Great Spirit lighted up the deep,
Where darkness had, for ages, had its keep,
And gave unto the light the name of Day;
The darkness He called Night, and that their
    sway
Might be divided, created, the fourth day,
The sun, and moon, and stars in bright array;
And set them in the firmament to light—
The sun the day, the lesser ones the night,
And they found wondrous favor in His sight.


The sun: that splendid, luminous, central sphere,
Sending to far off Neptune and planets near
Its white and radiant, warm and cheerful beams;
And through whose warmth and light the earth
    now gleams,

Reflecting back a beauty new and rare;
But there are none yet to behold it, there,
Except the Lord, who "saw that it was good,"
And all its use and beauty understood.
The penciled rays, through ether's vast expanse
Came warming and delighting with their glance.

The light created, now the perfect eye
Was made in God's own image, and, thereby,
The glory of the earth, and air, and sky,
And all created things that in them lie,
Were well perceived by man's immortal mind—
Each mirrored, by reflected light, in kind,
Through the transparent cornea, far behind
Into the picture gallery of the mind.

O, why did not the intellectual eye
As well discern lights of the mental sky?
Those great, bright lights sent hither to illume
The midnight darkness of the mental gloom
Which had, for ages, been the world's sad doom.
The great Gallileo, who sought to prove
The sun the center, and that earth did move,
Found recognition of these great truths slow,
And rack and torture had to undergo.
But when released from pain of inquisition,
Stoutly maintained his first and true position,
Determined that his light should brightly shine,
Though intolerance and ignorance should com-
    bine
By their opaqueness to shut out the line.

And they who first, by printing, thought to shed
A ray of light where all, it seemed, had fled,
And ignorance and darkness reigned supreme —
The hideous nightmare of a horrid dream —
And hoped to rend this dark and thick'ning veil,
And let the light of hope and truth prevail,
Were deemed, by superstitious minds, in league
With demons, in some new and dark intrigue.
These noble benefactors met, instead
Of love and homage, persecutions dread.
And yet this light shone brighter, on and on,
Dispelling the dark shadows, one by one,
Till knowledge, which so long had dormant lain
Through the Dark Ages, waked to life again:
Feeble its throbbings, first, but gaining strength
Until it grew, a Hercules, at length,
And ignorance — that heavy, galling chain
By which the Romish Popes had held full reign
O'er body and soul of man, in rule profane —
Could not 'gainst dawning light its sway maintain.
Like spectral shadows of the fallen foe
Upon the walls of Prague, were, long ago,
Dispelled, the legend says, by rising sun,
E'en so it was with this now glorious one.

Illustrious Luther gave once more to man
The Word of Light, which long, by fiendish clan,
Had been a fountain sealed, and quickly ran
The influence of this light through all the land,
Unchaining truth and right with mighty hand.
The Gospel of that wondrous Light that came

To be the light of men, eschewing fame
And Heaven's delights, that He might be to men
An everlasting Light and Glory, again,
The opaqueness of the mental eye removed,
Its vision thus restored and soon improved,
A great Illuminator warmed and glowed
Where long the stagnant stream of darkness
    flowed,
Brooded by vultures—man by man destroyed—
By ignorance divided and destroyed.
This reign of terror passed, the Light of Love
Shines for the hearts of all who round it move,
Irradiating wondrous fire and glow
To open hearts that long the truth to know.

But why, e'en yet, will some whom God has given
His glorious Light to guide their feet to heaven,
And perfect mental vision to behold
His goodness and His glories manifold,
Still let so many objects come between
Their souls and this One Great and Glorious
    Sheen,
Eclipsing all its brightness, and still walk
In darkened paths, where death and danger stalk?
Why still do ignorance and division tread
Life's highways—where the truth should reign
    instead?
For light, if not obstructed, ever brings
The perfect image of beholden things.
O, keep the soul and mind transparent, bright,
That God's own Word may there reflect the light.

## O NEVER AGAIN.

GONE is my youth and gladness —
  Gone is the wife of my heart!
I tread life's way with sadness
  And with longing to depart.

In years I am not old,
  But the joy of life is fled.
The hearth of home is cold,
  Its shining light is dead.

O never again, for me,
  Will a hearth glow as warm and bright;
And never again will I see
  Lamps that give out such light.

And never again shall I rest,
  This side of eternity,
As I did in the dear home-nest,
  Encouraged and soothed by thee.

Each joy was doubled by sharing —
  Each sorrow was lightened, too;
I could fight life's battles with daring,
  Helped by a smile from you.

But now I have no joys to share,
  And sorrows must bear alone;
I'm weary with life's fitful care —
  My once happy lot I bemoan.

O, why is there given such bliss,
　　So sweet but so short-lived,
If there's not a world beyond this,
　　Where we'll never be deprived

Of love, and rest, and home,
　　And all that makes life sweet?
Where never again we shall roam
　　With tired and lonely feet?


## MEMORIAL DAY.

THE day has come when we again
Strew flowers o'er our heroes slain;
And, with the garlands that we weave
For those for whom we sadly grieve,
Come memories of noble deeds —
The clash of arms, the neigh of steeds;
And once again our country bleeds,
As right with wrong so sternly pleads
In all dread warfare's rigid needs.

We hear once more the rousing call
For those who love their country, all,
Under her banner to enlist
To help dispel the rising mist
Which threatened to become a pall.
When —"Rally 'round the flag boys,"
Filled the village streets with noise;

Or, "Left, right! left, right!" sounding shrill,
As officers essayed to drill
Steps that hitherto had trod
In furrows made by fresh-turned clod,
Or, peacefully, their own green sod.

"To arms! to arms!" rang through the land,
And answering it, a loyal band
Came thronging, by the flag to stand.
Even the children caught the fire
Of patriotism and holy ire,
And rallied 'neath the colors dear,
With loyal songs and words of cheer;
Helping in others to inspire
Enthusiasm, and desire
To save the land at any price—
Even their lives the sacrifice.

With bayonets glistening in summer sun,
The last fond word and farewell done,
Father, husband, brother, friend,
And lover, now, their voices blend
In rousing cheers for native land,
And for the dear ones left behind.
And then we see them march away—
O, ever memorable day!
Their hearts high-beating at the thought
Of freedom won by battles fought;
They dash away the hasty tear,
To glance once more back to the rear
To catch the last hand wave of dear

21

And loving ones.   Again they cheer;
Seeking to drive away the fear
They see in the blanched faces, there,
Of mothers, wives, and sweethearts fair.
Proudly, sadly they march away,
Thinking of those they may never see;
The drum and fife sorrowf'ly play
"The Girl I Left Behind Me."
The terrors of war as yet unknown,
This was its first sad undertone —
Leaving their dear ones all alone.
The rallies, and dinners, and drill had been
Like a victor's march in triumphal din;
But now stern warfare they must face,
Till left no mark of treason's trace.


Village and farm left desolate —
This is war's too cruel fate.
The gray-haired man and fair-haired youth
Have gone to fight for home and truth;
And those in prime of hope and strength
Have gone, until there's left, at length,
Scarce one to guard the town from foes
That hold the border land in throes
Of fear and deep alarm: repose
Becomes a thing unknown to those
Weary and anxious women, who
Eagerly watch the coming through
Of the daily carrier of the news
From the seat of war.   He sadly views

The anxious group that gathers there,
Knowing the deep suspense and care
Gnawing their hearts; and feels a fear
Lest e'en the victory, bought so dear,
Of which he brings them word, may sear
The last fond hope; for some may hear
Of loved ones fallen on battled field,
And life to them no more shall yield
Aught but loneliness and grief.
The list of names is read in brief
And eager tones. "O God, 'tis true!"
A mother cries, "My boy in blue
In the front ranks has fallen, too!"
And, weeping, she falls upon the breast
Of the gentle girl whom he loved best;
Together they mingle their tears and moan
For a life that was dearer to both than their own.
A wife, with eager and pallid face,
In missing or wounded list can trace,
E'en through her tears, the name of him
Without whose love life seemed so dim;
She looks in wondering baby eyes,
So like to his, and bravely tries
To summon courage to endure
The dread suspense she cannot cure.
"Wounded or missing, dying or dead:"
This was what the papers said —
And life was o'er for those who read.

O War! dark vulture brooding o'er
Hearts and homes where, e'er before,

Love, and hope, and light had lent
A charm to life; ere treason rent
Our glorious land with dark intent!
But, at length, the cloud is past—
The Union saved; and now, at last,
They who are left betake their way
Homeward—impatient at delay.
But O the thousands of proud, brave men
Who never came back to their homes again!
And O how many have died, since then,
From health that was weakened in prison pen,
Or by exposure and hardened fare
That surrounds the soldier everywhere!

Strew flowers—strew flowers of brightest hue
Over the graves of our heroes true!
Fire the guns and muffle the drums!
Check not the tear that quickly comes,
As memories of our noble slain
Come thronging in a golden train!
Let young and old, in one acclaim,
Attest the honor and the fame
In which we hold the soldier's name:
They whose lives were sanctified
Through love of country—noble pride!
And while we lay our offerings down—
Tokens of love and true renown—
May God give an eternal crown!

## OUR COUNTRY.

"Our country, 'tis of thee,"
    We proudly sing!
For thy prosperity
    Best wishes bring!
Blest be thy liberty —
    Each man a king!


There lies beneath the sun
    No fairer land
Than this, our loved one —
    United band
Of loyal States, begun
    By justice's hand.


May it no more be rent
    By aught of ill;
But, to its lustre, lent
    Each noble thrill
Of loyal hearts, content
    With country still.


And as, in days of yore,
    Sweet liberty
Was prized as naught before,
    E'en so may we
Lay up, in royal store,
    Its dignity:

Teach all our boys and girls
  Its worth to prize;
And as our flag unfurls
  Free to the skies,
So let their thoughts—bright pearls—
  For freedom rise.

"Our country, 'tis of thee,"
  We sing to-day!
Thou art so great and free!—
  For thee we pray,
That *free* thou'lt ever be,
  And blest thy sway!

And vast eternity
  Shall catch the ray
Of light shed out by thee
  For eternal day!
God bless our country, free!—
  For this we pray.

JULY 4, 1886.


## WRECK OF THE STEAMER SULTANA.
### APRIL 26, 1865.

AT the wharf at Memphis the steamer lay,
Illum'ed by the sunlight's glistening ray,
At nearly the close of a sweet spring day.
  In power, and beauty, and grace,
  A magnificent floating palace—
The pride and pomp of the river's array.

And crowded on the decks around,
Two thousand soldiers, homeward bound,
With weakened health, and many a wound,
    Stand watching the setting sun,
    Thinking, ere many a one
Has set, the "welcome home" shall sound.


The wished for hour has come at last—
Seiges and battles are things of the past;
No more will they march at the bugle's blast,
    But be free to resume, once more,
    The pursuits of the years before—
Ere the dark cloud of war its shadow cast.


How good it seems to be free again—
Free from the Southern prison pen—
Free to act and think as men.
    And a hope beams in the eye,
    As they watch the sunset sky,
Of seeing home and friends again.


And many happy words are spoken
That all the joy of hope betoken;
And thus the tiresome delay is broken.
    The sun at last is down,
    And brilliant lights of the town
Shed out their gleaming ray unbroken.


At length the crew have sought repose,
And, wrapt in slumber, dream of those

So dear to them.   Now onward goes
   The great boat, glidingly
   And majestically,
Bearing its precious freight of heroes.

Enjoy thy dreams, O soldier true,
'Tis all that's left for thee to do!—
The joy that's permeating through
   The happy, throbbing brow
   Will be the last—for now,
Death, instead of home, awaits you.

A loud explosion rends the air—
More terrible than cannons are!
And now confusion, wild, reigns where
   So peacefully they dreamed
   That almost home they seemed;
And all is horror and dark despair.

The water is covered with a writhing mass—
A wounded, helpless, drowning mass—
And the boats are all blown away.   Alas!
   The hope that fanned their dreams
   A mocking phantom seems—
For now it can never come to pass.

Some struggle wildly with despair,
And shrieks for help now rend the air,
But all in vain—no help is there.
   The boat that proudly came
   Is now all wreathed in flame,
Shedding on the scene a lurid glare.

And they who oft had faced death where
The bullets whistled through the air,
With bitter cry of offered prayer,
 Leap from the burning boat;
 But the waters only gloat,
And close again o'er a prey so fair.

The balmy morning dawns, at last,
But the struggle for life has long been past;
The soldiers awake not—their eyes are fast
 Closed in that dreamless sleep,
 In their couch in the watery deep—
Waiting the call of the last trumpet's blast.

Of all who had watched the setting sun,
With thoughts of home now almost won,
How few are left to hail this one!
 Nearer home than they thought—
 All of life's battles fought
In this, their last, hard, desperate one!

The "Father of Waters" thy shroud and thy grave,
Sleep peacefully under the dark, turbid wave,
O soldiers, true-hearted, enduring and brave!

## LITTLE THINGS.

The angry word that's said in haste
 Seems but a little thing;
But O the heart 's a burning waste
 Embittered by its sting.

22

The careless word of gossip's tongue,
  Unheeding where it falls,
May break the finest friendship 'mong
  Those whom its venom thralls.

The wine-cup raised to boyish lips
  Is thought a trivial thing;
But 'tis not long ere fiery sips
  Death and destruction bring.

One glass too much with friends imbibed
  Robbed a nation of her king; —
The history, for years inscribed,
  Changed by this little thing.

The first wrong step quickly retraced
  Would little trouble bring;
But if pursued, soon is effaced
  The way to true living.

A kindly word, or look, or tone,
  Given to hearts that bleed,
Soothes many a care and bitter moan;
  And supplements their need.

The few things learned each day we live,
  And treasured up as small,
Do, in the end, much knowledge give,
  And pave the way to all.

Each tempter foiled, each victory won,
  Gives strength to win again:

We fight life's battles one by one,
   On mountain top or fen.

O can we call these little things,
   That sway a nation's fate?
Or to our lives so surely bring
   A joy or woe so great?

There is no Lilliputian scale
   For seeming little things;
For each one is a knight in mail,
   Which shame or honor brings.


## ACROSS THE FIELDS.

Across the fields of life we stray
   Gathering golden grain;
Gleaming and winnowing every day,
   Some treasure new to gain.

The stubble, though bright, is rough to our feet,
   As we follow the reapers' train,
Gathering up the golden wheat,
   The bread of life to gain.

Hard must we glean in the fields of thought
   Under the harvest sun,
Gath'ring up where others have wrought,
   Winnowing when day is done.

And many handfuls of golden grain
 Are left, by reapers kind,
To cheer and gladden the weary brain
 Of the industrious mind.

Let us glean, too, in the harvest of souls,
 Seeking if we may bring
Even one of our comrades, out of the shoals,
 Unto the Harvest King.


## GENIUS.

Just as the artist catches every shade
And richly-tinted coloring of the sky,
And makes them live again on glowing canvas,—
Even so the poet-artist must imbibe
And catch each light and shade of passing feel-
 ing;
Each longing aspiration and each sigh
At failures; each bounding throb of gladsome
 rapture
When high success has crowned the laboring oar;
The shout, the silent tear, the laugh, the moan—
He should depict it all as if his own
Heart beat with fever heat with all the world.

His ear should catch the music high above
The harsh, discordant notes of lower air,
And in melodious measures sing it o'er
To fellow mortals struggling on the way.

His eyes should note all beauty, everywhere,
Of spirit, or of earth and air and sky;
And he should then interpret it to man,
In words that burn and glow with heavenly fire.


## HOMESICK.

IF childhood could come again,
  With its long, bright afternoons;
The orchard, and home, and mother;
  The restful, quiet moons—
How quickly our cares would vanish,
  And heal the deep heart wounds.

If only again we could saunter
  Down the shady path to the well,
Or through the leafy orchard
  Where we loved to sit so well,
How much of life's hard burden
  We'd roll off—who can tell?

O the dear, old-fashioned home,
  So full of rest and peace!
To thee we would gladly come,
  And gain a sweet surcease
From cares, which, with the years,
  Alarmingly increase.

O rosy, care-free childhood!
  No poet's pen can paint

Thy free and happy pleasures,
  Before the world's restraint
Has harshened the sweet measures
  By its sad, selfish taint.


## WHEN LIFE IS O'ER.

LIFE's "fitful fever o'er,"
We will no more deplore
The endless woes in store
  For mortals here.

We'll leave all harrowing care,
And dwell forever where
God's loved and just ones are
  When life is over.

When we shall live anew,
The good we sought to do
But did not carry through
  Will then appear.

All will be understood—
The "why" of bad and good,
If just the best we could
  We wrought while here.

And heart shall speak to heart;
And ne'er be torn apart
By doubt, or angry dart
  Of passion's whim.

Life's "fitful fever o'er,"
God grant that we may soar
To realms where, evermore,
We'll rest in peace.


## A BOUNDLESS OCEAN.

THE world is a boundless ocean—
  Like little boats we ride,
Driven, by circumstances,
  In and out with the tide.


We never know when we're happy—
  Life's pleasures seem greatest when past;
Tossed hither and yon by the breakers,
  We're engulfed by a maelstrom at last.


Would we could sail o'er life's ocean
  In ships all iron-clad,
Pouring oil on troubled waters—
  Smiling, however sad!


Ruling, not succumbing,
  The angry waves of fate;
And, by noble, steady doing,
  Make our lives consecrate!

## A SONG.

LIFE has nothing worth giving
    But love.
'Twould not be worth living
    'Thout love.
There's naught so refining,
So free from repining,
So like stars a-shining,
    As love.

*Chorus:* Love, love, blest love—
    Life has nothing worth giving
        But love.
    Life has nothing worth giving—
    'Twould not be worth living—
    'Twould not be worth living
        'Thout love.

There is nothing worth seeking
    But love,
Through all the worlds eking
    'Tis love.
Fond hearts close combining,
Kin souls thus entwining—
Brings richest heart-mining:
    Sweet love!

There is naught up in heaven
    But love;
The Rock that was riven
    Was love.

And there we'll be given
A love pure as heaven —
Our sins all forgiven
     Through love.


## LABORERS WITH GOD.

FOR we are "laborers with God,"
   The great mosaic, soul, to build;
We should make life a masterpiece
   When aided by so high a guild.


God's not in need of our poor aid,
   But stoops to help *us* as we build:
Let us be guided by His law —
   His hand than ours is much more skilled.


Be careful how and where we build —
   Make the great structure strong and pure;
Build on the true Foundation Stone,
   That it in beauty shall endure
When tried by deep adversity —
   The fire, and rain, and heavy storm.
If planned by the Great Architect,
   'Twill stand in whiter, cleaner form.

23

## GROWING.

THE growing flower needs the sun,
　Its fragrant beauty to unfold;
And in our lives must shine God's love,
　Their grace and usefulness to mold.

The plant needs wind and rain, as well—
　Daylight and darkness, dew and shade;
And so by trials hard to bear
　Our souls are often stronger made.

God leads us often through the sea,
　Or o'er the desert's burning sand,
That by this schooling we may gain
　The power to "possess the land."

Then let us murmur not at fate—
　Contented be, whate'er betide;
If only we at last may meet
　Our Savior on the other side.

## CLEPSYDRA.

THE water steals away
Through the ancient clepsydra,
As the fleeting moments stray;
The notches, that tell the hours
On the stick, as the water lowers,
Show us time's passing hours.

Our life, too, steals away
Through Time's great clepsydra —
It's drops we cannot stay.
There are notches that tell the hours,
The fresh or the withered flowers —
The strong or the failing powers.

We know when it is the morn
By the brimming hope, new-born,
That all will be oil and corn
And love along life's highway,
And brilliant will be the day,
As the waters glide away.

When half empty is the jar,
And doubt and sorrow mar
Our once most brilliant star,
We know it is high noon
Come to our lives too soon,
Ere half solved the mystic rune.

Children to men have grown!
And one by one have flown
Old friends — their graves are strewn
With tears and flowers sweet;
And here and there we meet
Another, with tired feet,

Like us grown old and gray,
His life fast slipping away
Toward its closing day;

And we know the eve draws near.
Happy, if we may hear
The hour sound strong and clear.*


## BE GENTLE.

O CURB the self-assertion
    That rises quick and strong—
'Tis not the right nutrition
    For love and peace at home.

The angry word will linger
    And in each bosom burn,
Like bite of pois'nous stinger,
    In the atmosphere of home.

And it will bring no sooner
    The recognition sought;
For love and justice, ever,
    By gentleness are brought.

And sweeter far than honey
    To the hearts of those we love—
Better than fame or money—
    Will the soft answer prove.

O guard the priceless treasure—
    The love within your home;
And do not stint its measure
    Or let its brightness gloam,

---

* Some of the wealthier ancients had clepsydras which sounded a musical note each hour,

Through lack of kindly favor
  And gentle patient tone.
He who is slow to anger
  Rules on the highest throne.

In all this wide world over
  Let us make one spot so dear,
That our souls shall find safe harbor
  From storms of doubt and fear.


## NOW, AND THEN.

THE things of life seem wonderfully small,
Compared to those beyond—and why enthrall
Our minds and hearts by making them our all?

What though success our efforts does not crown
With joy, or love, or pittance of renown,
If, at the last, we gain a heavenly crown?

What though our eager hands do fail to grasp
The laurel, and unfinished is our task,
If but, at last, our Savior's hand we clasp?

What though our hearts are often sore oppressed
In this short life, and anguish fill the breast,
If, in the great hereafter, we gain rest?

What though our longing eyes may fail to see
The consummation of our aims, if we
May win, for work, heaven's vast eternity?

What though by adverse winds our lives be driven,
And on time's rocky coast be sadly riven,
If we but anchor safe, at last, in heaven?

Love, fame, wealth and earthly ease —
O we can well afford to lose all these,
If fanned our brows, at last, by heaven's breeze.